Bring out the

Genius

in your Child

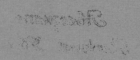

hamlyn

Bring out the ● Genius

in your Child

Fun activities to stretch young minds from **0 – 11 years**

Ken Adams

Contents

First published in Great Britain in 2006
by Hamlyn, a division of Octopus Publishing
Group Ltd, 2–4 Heron Quays, London E14 4JP

Copyright © Octopus Publishing Group Ltd
2006

This material was previously published as
Bring out the Genius in your Child.

Distributed in the United States and
Canada by Sterling Publishing Co., Inc.
387 Park Avenue South, New York,
NY 10016–8810

ISBN-13: 978-0-600-61435-7
ISBN-10: 0-600-61435-2

A CIP catalogue record for this book
is available from the British Library

Printed and bound in China

10 9 8 7 6 5 4 3 2 1

Introduction

Three months ago, Stuart was in a remedial set at school. He could hardly read, his mathematics was at a rudimentary level and, on the face of it, he was a slow learner destined for bottom sets in the secondary school and continued failure. But, after working with him for an hour, I became convinced that, far from being a slow learner, he was able to learn fast if he was properly motivated. Giving his parents advice on how to help him in between my visits, I returned twice a week to work with Stuart. Soon his English and maths improved dramatically.

Now, Stuart reads well, writes stories that are extremely good and imaginative, and has dramatically improved his spelling. He can add, subtract, do long multiplication and division and can problem-solve. He has also been moved out of his remedial set.

Like Stuart, other very bright, fast-learning children can be motivated to fulfil their highest potential, because the state-of-the-art learning methods you will meet in this book ensure that learning is fast and effective for all abilities.

Armed with the knowledge of these learning methods and how to motivate children as explained in this book, you can encourage children over a wide range of ages and abilities. As a parent helping with your child's schoolwork you are in a unique position. You know your child as no one else does. This book will give you guidance throughout pre-school and primary school, and using this unique knowledge will enable your child to fulfil his or her intellectual potential, and iron out difficulties with schoolwork that may arise.

This book ensures that learning is fast and effective for all abilities.

Failure will certainly become a forgotten word, and, who knows, you could be bringing out the genius in your child.

Ken Adams

How children learn

1

The creation of mental images

When the senses – sight, hearing, taste, touch and smell – receive exterior 'signals', the receptors in the sense organs – eyes, ears, taste buds, skin and nose – stimulate nerves which pass impulses to the brain. Looking at a word or sum written on a page, for example, forms an image in the retina of the eye. Receptors in the retina are stimulated, and nerve impulses pass along the optic nerve to the brain. These impulses are specific to that word or sum and, so that an attempt at recognition can be made next time it is encountered, the impulses are encoded.

When looking at a specific item we view a 'scene', so there must be some selective process that eliminates items that we do not wish to consider. Many failures in academic learning occur because learning material has not been presented in a way that isolates specific ideas or concepts, or because concentration is not sufficient to create appropriate images and develop understanding.

The encoded impulses are passed on to a short-term memory that can hold them for up to several minutes while a search or scan of more extensive long-term memory is made for something similar. At this point, if concentration falters and different information is encoded, it can 'displace' the preceding information from short-term memory.

The nature of images

In order to compare accurately the incoming information, now held in short-term memory, with various items from long-term memory, we create mental images. A child looking at a word, after encoding it, translates it into a mental-image presentation of the word. How alike the actual word and the mental image are is a matter of conjecture, but there are great similarities between how we all 'see' things. Usually, if we view a real-life object such as a house, a car or a street, then its mental representation is a clear three-dimensional picture. Abstracts, such as the word 'justice', do not create clear pictures, but rather images of associated behaviour, perhaps a judge in a wig pronouncing judgement or a famous court case.

To create meaning, there must be some form of close-matching of the image of what we see with something in long-term memory. Creating a range of images from memory and attempting to match or near-match with the image of what enters our sense organs are attempts to give meaning to what we see, hear or feel.

An exact match

If the image of what we see matches exactly with something in our memory, we know exactly what it is. We recognize a house, a street, a word

The learning system

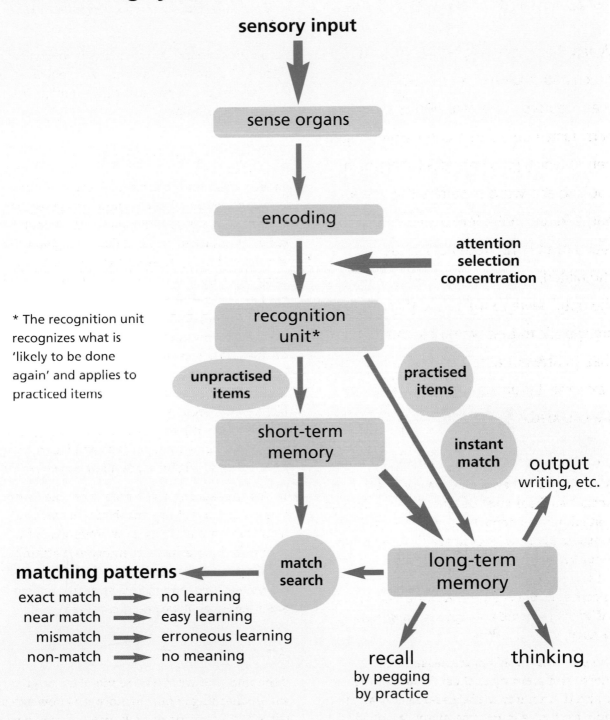

sensory input

sense organs

encoding

attention
selection
concentration

recognition
unit*

* The recognition unit recognizes what is 'likely to be done again' and applies to practiced items

unpractised items

practised items

short-term memory

instant match

output
writing, etc.

matching patterns ← match search ← long-term memory

exact match → no learning
near match → easy learning
mismatch → erroneous learning
non-match → no meaning

recall
by pegging
by practice

thinking

or a multiplication sum and have an exact match. Sometimes, if we have seen the image many times before, there may be an instant match. Then, even the creation of images from memory is bypassed and recognition is through matching of codes. This is when rehearsal or practice has repeated the item so often that the code is recognized by a recognition unit that has been primed because 'this is likely to be done again'. Practising something to this point, even beyond the point where we know the answer really well, is called overlearning – we become skilled, as with recall of the answer in a times table.

Exact matches represent contact with a secure world. We know what we see and understand it perfectly. However, simply repeating familiar experiences that we know does not allow us to learn. A well-learned times table, even if your child's level of understanding is that 3 x 10 means three lots of ten cars added together, is useful as a means to further learning – division and cancelling in fractions, for example. Simply repeating the experience, though, will not further learning. Knowledge is not increased by an overfamiliar environment, where similar experiences are repeated. Overfamiliarity can limit mind-building and, ultimately, also limit thinking and creative ability.

Near or close matches

When the environment continuously throws up new and challenging experiences they can modify previous experience, expanding opportunities to learn. If what enters our sense organs is not too different from what is in long-term memory, there is a near match which modifies that related part of memory. For example, in memory you have the generalized idea of a house, a tree or a street. When you see a street, a type of tree or a type of house that you have never seen before, you take note of the modifications to the generalized concept, moving from the general idea to the specific. In addition, the modifications are labelled: the new tree is, perhaps, a beech tree; the new street is perhaps West Street and can be tied to a town, a location, and a time when it was visited.

Learning is easy if the new experience is close to something in the memory. However, children vary in their ability to modify the concepts in their minds. Slow-learning pupils often find it difficult to near-match learning material with experience in their memory. In areas like reading, numbers, algebra, mechanics and problem-solving, if they are introduced to new work that is too remote from what they know they will not be able to achieve near-matching. In other words, what for one pupil is a near match, for another can be a non-match. The answer is to stage work carefully, producing close matches, closer than the near match that sustains the learning of the average learner. When this is done, slow learners learn with ease. Without such structuring, as time progresses, they can be left stranded at an attainment level that is further and further below that of quick learners.

Non-matching

Non-matching is met with frequently during the learning process. If work is organized and graded to the needs of the learner, learning should be a positive experience without failures. A child will move on from step one to step two with ease through near or close matches. Unfortunately, sometimes textbooks and certain systems of learning have been carelessly compiled or have a philosophical background that neglects structure in learning.

Also, if you present material to a child, you must be sure that there is something similar in his memory to modify. If there is not, then the new experience has no meaning, and will be, for the child, like attempting to understand hieroglyphics. To avoid a non-match situation, testing is necessary so that an appropriate level of matching is found in whatever is being learned. This is not as rigid as it sounds. It is true that certain areas of learning must be learned before others. The learning of counting, for example, must come before addition – to reverse this sequence is a logical impossibility – and it is important that you discover these prerequisites where they occur (they litter the learning of mathematics in particular).

Mismatching

The system of searching for meaning through the matching of mental images is a relatively slow process of recognition. It is a fine-tuning system that can consider possible meanings by throwing up a variety of possible matches from memory. Sometimes, though, lack of appropriate knowledge, or incompletely learned areas of knowledge, can lead to a situation where a child (or an adult) can assign wrong meaning to something. The learner in this case has little in his memory which is similar to what is being learned, and therefore matches the nearest thing he can find, rather than non-matching and assigning no meaning to it. Consequently, wrong meanings are often given to words, processes in maths, principles in science, in problem-solving and so on. Mismatching leads to loss of confidence in one's own thinking, but can be completely eliminated if the two principles of near-matching and sequencing, described above, are carefully followed.

Landmarks

At particular ages children normally reach certain landmarks and should be able to complete certain matches, and these are summarized below.

- **Aged 2–3** Your child won't really understand what numbers signify. Although he may be able to count, he will probably get the order of the numbers confused – particularly numbers above ten.

- **Aged 3–4** He should be able to count by now, but won't be capable of thinking of numbers in abstract terms and can only recognize groups of three items or fewer. He will probably enjoy board games (without any strategy being involved) and factual books, in which he likes to see what happens as you read to him. He may also like expounding his own theories and getting you to explain things to him.

- **Aged 4–5** He will begin to comprehend comparative numbers (that two is smaller than three, but bigger than one) and should be able to sort items by now. For instance, he should be capable of sorting the laundry into white items and coloured ones, and of putting cutlery on the table for each person. He may also have an awareness that different people have different opinions.

- **Aged 6–7** He may now begin to employ basic strategies when playing games. Ordering objects by size, and simple addition, should also be within his grasp.

Recalling information

Children often achieve clear understanding of a concept or subject, but a short time later seem to have forgotten all they were taught. It may be assumed that they have a bad memory, but with proper understanding of how to memorize subjects they can recall information perfectly. The two distinct ways to help with recalling information – practice and pegging – are valuable tools.

Practice

Practice well beyond the point where we feel that we know something – overlearning – achieves bypassing of the image-matching system from short-term memory. Somewhere between the sensory system and short-term memory there is recognition of the possibility of further repetition, and this is only primed after extensive practice sessions. Matching then occurs instantaneously between coded information in the memory and that from the sense organs and the match is an exact one – we know exactly what it is.

There is effective practice for children to achieve overlearning, and there is ineffective practice. Mindlessly repeating items, so-called rote learning, is not only an irksome process, it is also an inefficient one. Conscious attempts at visualization can achieve in a fraction of the time exactly what rote achieves.

Visualizing what you practise is a way of screaming louder at the recognition unit, 'I have a match! I have a match! Put me in your instant code recognition system!' Eventually, the recognition unit complies, and takes the overlearned item under its wing.

Learning of this type is a skill, and always involves superficial learning – how to drive a car or repeat times tables. The answer to 3 x 5 is learned by rote, but the deeper meaning of 'three fives are fifteen' goes through the visualization system, because the answer to 'What does three fives are fifteen mean in real-life terms?' demands a mental image of three groups of five. It is an exact match, but takes a little more time to produce. For learning, this aspect of times tables is more important than the mere skill aspect, because of the possible modifications that can be made.

Pegging

This method of effecting recall involves the use of mental 'pegs'. To recall a town or a street, for example, you can attach the experience of that place to the firmly established 'line of time' that ticks away in your memory. On such a day, at such a time you visited that place. To strengthen the pegging, the street or town has a name, and also has an attachment to the knowledge of other places, roads, and so on that you have mapped into memory. Also, you have a story to tell: 'At 7.30 a.m. my alarm woke me. I dressed and had beans on toast for breakfast. Then I got the car out of the garage and followed the motorway to...' Multi-pegging of this type makes recall of visits to places very good indeed.

Pegging

2 piles of sticks,
26 sticks and 15 sticks

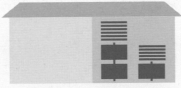

2 bundles of 10 sticks
and 1 bundle of 10 sticks

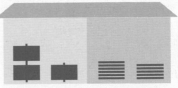

3 bundles of ten moved
6 and 5 loose sticks left

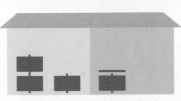

10 loose sticks bundled
together

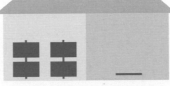

last bundle of 10 moved
1 single stick left

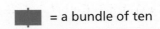 = a bundle of ten

4 bundles of 10 and
1 single = 41

Such pegging is a mechanism for survival in the real world. In schoolwork, the preferred method of memorization has always been practice, probably because the initiation of practice is easy – the experience is simply repeated. Pegging is a quicker way to achieve recall, but for someone inexperienced in developing pegs a certain amount of mental effort is required.

Learning to count is an example of an area that is practised and also extensively pegged.

> One, two, buckle my shoe,
> Three, four, knock at the door,
> Five, six, pick up sticks,
> Seven, eight, lay them straight,
> Nine, ten, a big fat hen.

Numbers are pegged to real-life objects in this rhyme, and also to the sense of rhythm. The rhyme also has the elements and form of a story.

Processes and operations can also be pegged. For example, the minute hand of a clock may be imagined moving clockwise for addition, anticlockwise for subtraction.

Using the form of a story can peg fairly complicated processes in memory. For 'carrying' in addition, the process can be perfectly pegged by imagining a man picking up sticks in a barn.

The sum we want to work out is:
$$\begin{array}{r} 26 \\ + 15 \\ \hline 41 \end{array}$$

In the illustration above a man has collected the two piles of sticks on the right-hand side. There are more than ten, so he has made bundles of tens and taken them to the left side, leaving the odd ones on the right. He now has six sticks and five sticks left over, so he makes another bundle of ten. Leaving the one stick on the right-hand side, he carries the single bundle of ten on the left and adds it to the others.

The advantage of using this format over practical work is that the near match is close enough to provide a modifying link between the concrete and the abstract. Animating the concept in the form of an illustration helps the process of close-matching what is to be learned with what is in the memory.

Thinking and creativity

So far, this chapter has concerned itself with matching between input (what enters through the sense organs) and what is in the memory. Creative thinking, on the other hand, is concerned with modifications within the mind, when one concept modifies another through mental effort, or even spontaneously.

Creative thinking

This will clearly depend on the number of concepts and groups of knowledge in our memory, and on our ability to search for 'links' between them. Rigid thinking can result in patterns of thought being repeated endlessly and new links being rejected as an invasion of a secure view of the world.

Creative thinking can be stimulated by certain types of problem-solving (divergent thinking) and also by adventurous output. Such output can be expressed through a variety of avenues – creative writing, artwork, model making, mathematical and scientific investigations, and philosophical discourse.

Problem-solving

Some types of problem-solving are creative. Divergent problem-solving asks for several possible answers to a question: 'What are the benefits for an earthworm of living in a wood?' Convergent problem-solving asks for a single answer: 'I am four times as old as my son. In twelve years' time, I shall be twice as old as him. How old am I now?' Convergent problem-solving requires a dissection into component parts, solving those parts, and then piecing together the solutions to achieve a single final solution. Strategies to problem-solve such as trial and error or algebraic formulae can be learned, and follow the learning-by-modification system of general learning. Strategies can also be practised or pegged.

There is also the element of sequencing. Problem-solving can be taught by progressing from problems with one sum to be solved to problems with several. The simplest example corresponds to the general concept, and near-matching can build into memory progressively more complex problem-solving techniques.

What time will it be in 30 minutes?

Convergent learning

Half-past 4!

Learning sequences

Matching newly learnt material with experience and building concept on concept forms a learning sequence. Certain concepts are without doubt prerequisites to others. Counting, for example, must come before addition or subtraction. However the sequencing of other concepts, such as talking and reading, aren't as clearly defined and may differ from child to child.

Finding sequences

To find sequences within learning is important, and each sequence must be thoroughly learned. Reading, for example, is a composite learning exercise, and there are several starting points. However, to achieve reading success each starting point and each component of reading must be learned completely otherwise progress falters.

Whether learning to talk should come before learning to read is debatable. One boy of ten months learned to read words and understand their meanings as he learned to talk – the reading of words simply gave him more to talk about. Usually, though, children learn to talk well before learning to read.

Word meanings

With word meanings the general concept is learned before the specific: for example, a child usually learns about trees in general before learning about pine trees in particular. However, if he has lived in a pine forest since birth, his general concept of a tree will have the shape and basic features of a pine. When he meets new trees, he modifies the 'pine concept to include them and their 'pegging' names. This can lead to error, because his general concept of a tree has cones and is evergreen. He has to re-learn the fact that not all trees are evergreen and have cones. Ideally, the general concept is learned by looking at a wide variety of trees and finding what they have in common, then being specific, such as dividing them into evergreens and deciduous.

School learning is littered with areas where sequencing would speed understanding, particularly in maths. Many of the exercises in this book have been sequenced to make learning easier.

What can I cook with cheese?

Macaroni cheese!

Divergent learning

Cheese on toast!

Cheese sandwich!

Motivating your child

However well learning material is organized, and practice, pegging and output are developed, it is to no avail if a child will not focus on what needs to be learned. The ability to concentrate and sustained motivation and interest are vital.

Concentration

Good concentration is achieved through clear presentation of concepts in as uncluttered an environment as possible; through confidence; through motivational factors such as short-term rewards, long-term rewards and interest; and through visualization techniques that use all the senses. Writing, drawing, painting, talking and dramatization about what is being learned can also increase concentration: for example, you draw a picture to illustrate a principle, or copy out a spelling word.

The way that learning material is presented is of prime importance for concentration. The ability to concentrate on something is directly related to the quality of mental image that is produced from it. Once a clear image of a concept has been produced it facilitates exact- and near-matching, and helps to reduce the incidence of mismatches. Presenting ideas in a clear form without distractions, through clear diagrams and pictures, and larger letters for the early stages of reading are helpful, but exceptional imaging can be achieved through a multi-sensory approach. Learning a letter or word by tracing it in a sand tray as well as

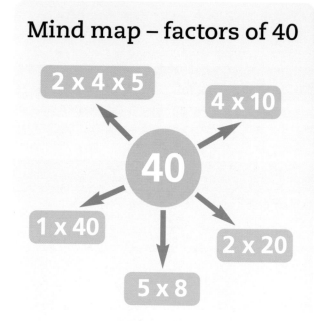

Mind map – factors of 40

2 x 4 x 5

4 x 10

40

1 x 40

2 x 20

5 x 8

seeing it and saying it draws on more senses and helps it to stick in the mind. Closing one's eyes and trying to visualize something also deepens concentration and visualization. Ideas, words and principles can also be 'webbed' (Mind Mapped©) to isolate them, so that their inner structure can be examined. In spelling, for example, this technique can be used to put words into similarly structured groups or to separate them.

Motivation

In the perfect world, wanting to learn would be enough to motivate your child. In the real world, without the drive to look carefully at a problem, to examine a diagram or read a book, there is little opportunity for learning to take place.

Much motivation comes from easy learning, so presentation, sequencing, and making matches results in a greater readiness to learn.

But what if a child will not even begin to attend to learning? Giving children a choice between playing sport and problem-solving often leaves problem-solving a poor second; and most children would prefer a fairground ride to a page of sums. Hopefully, such a direct choice can be avoided where learning is concerned, and rather the fairground ride is offered as an inducement to work hard: 'I'll take you to the fair if you learn how to do these division sums.' A break with a favourite drink or food, or perhaps: 'You can watch that TV programme when you've finished' are other inducements.

Often, parental approval is enough. Most children wish to please their parents, and motivation can be strong if, mingled with the confidence that they will succeed, is the slight hint that tells a child that if they do not even try, they may fall short of expectations. That small, almost imperceptible surge of adrenalin can almost always focus attention. It is a parent's responsibility to manage this delicate balance intelligently and with compassion, because too much stress is a powerful inhibitor.

Even greater motivation develops when everyone around the child – her parents, school and society – rates success in education very highly. Then there is the motivation of long-term rewards of an elevated position in society, and the financial status and esteem that such a position brings with it.

Interest

Making learning interesting can be certainly sufficient motivation in itself, but educators must also be aware of the constraints of time, the curriculum and the principles of learning. Trying to make the pages of workbooks interesting by adding many illustrations, for instance, may so clutter up the space that clear presentation of a concept may be destroyed, and will defeat the object. Using a computer game format to teach an unappetizing area of maths will very often heighten interest but may teach very little if the game rather than the maths is the primary concern of the programmer.

Encouraging creativity in children will in turn boost their self-esteem and promote greater success in learning, so interesting them in creative activities is another sound strategy.

How to enhance your child's concentration

- Select a quiet area of the house for learning activities: television, radio and the noise of other people will only distract her. And stay nearby yourself to encourage her.

- When you want her to do something, say her name at the start of the relevant sentence and make eye contact. This will grab her attention and make her more responsive to what you are saying.

- Make sure that any potential distractions, such as toys and demanding siblings, are out of reach or otherwise occupied.

- When you've said something important to your child, ask her to repeat it in order to reinforce the point. Moving closer to her when you speak is another good idea.

Learning with your baby 0–1 Year

2

Developing perception

Babies demonstrate an amazing ability and desire to learn and make sense of the world around them right from birth. Babies learn to discern contrasts in voices very quickly and can recognise their mother's voice and face from an early stage. Babies can also discriminate sound patterns, including melodies and speech inflections, soon after birth. Tiffany, a baby of five weeks, learned to repeat her aunt's high-pitched 'Hello!' in perfect imitation. At ten weeks she also learned to say 'Mother'. It took many repetitions, day after day, as she clearly copied sounds and the movement of her aunt's lips, until she had it exactly right.

The widening world

There is a thirtyfold increase in the visual activity of the adult compared to that of the newborn child. Only those stimuli seen most clearly will attract a baby's attention. Newborn babies can only see things up to about 50 cm (20 in) away. They can detect black and white stripes about 30 cm (12 in) away if the stripes are no less than around 2 cm (¾ in) wide – otherwise everything is a blur. They see their mother's face as three-dimensional and can recognize it because of the light contrast in the face (the eyes, mouth and hairline stand out), the voice and inflections, touch and smell.

Newborn babies prefer movement to stationary objects or people, three-dimensional to two-dimensional items, high contrast to low contrast, and curved to straight lines.

By three months, they have learned about object coherence and unity, and the crawling stage broadens experience of shape and form

Abilities present at birth

- Basic sensory capacities
- Colour vision
- Hearing, particularly those sensitive to the range of the human voice
- Sound patterns

- Smelling, tasting and senses of touch and motion are also well developed
- Depth perception developed by three months, picture cues by five to seven months
- From the age of three months babies learn to appreciate that objects exist even when moved out of sight

dramatically through touching, rolling and tumbling. As soon as they reach out for things and are rewarded by a learning experience, they begin to modify their areas of knowledge.

At six months babies are able to grasp a wooden block and sit up. A few months later, they are able to crawl. With each successive stage of physical development comes the ability to investigate new areas of their world and develop new knowledge in their memory to which further knowledge can be linked. The more they know, the greater is the potential. Of course it is worth bearing in mind that some babies will learn faster than others, as do children and adults.

The more varied and extensive the number of experiences your baby has, the greater the knowledge that develops. Many experiences come in the natural course of bringing up a baby – contact with body surfaces during feeding, the touch of a bottle, the texture and smell of the blankets on the bed, the shapes and patterns in changing light about the cot and pram.

Development skills

A baby's skills develop rapidly during the first year, as shown in the table below.

- **3 months**
  Reaches out towards objects that are close at hand and tries to grab them; is able to hold her head up for longer periods of time, whether lying on her front or back; expresses her moods through an increasing variety of facial expressions; responds to distinctive noises and falls quiet on hearing a small sound; can distinguish a man from a woman by their face.

- **6 months**
  Uses her fingers to put food to her mouth in an attempt to feed herself; can sit up on her own without being supported in any way; recognizes her name and responds to it by turning; screams when feeling angry, gurgles when playing and laughs when contented; recognizes herself in the mirror and can even recognize herself in a photograph.

- **9 months**
  Is capable of pointing to an item she is attracted to; makes stepping movements when supported under the arms; shows curiosity about other babies and may even poke them; may be able to copy any animal noises that you make; waves back if someone else waves to her.

- **12 months**
  Is able to pour water from a container held in either hand; can climb up the stairs without difficulty; demonstrates affection for other members of the family; recognizes the names of other family members; can follow simple instructions such as 'Wave goodbye'.

Talking to your baby

Much of your baby's first year is concerned with physical development – reaching, grasping, sitting, crawling, walking – in order to explore the limits of a secure environment. Imitating sounds is a big part of that experimentation and should be encouraged by talking to your baby at every opportunity.

Encouraging speech

When you put your face close to your baby and say a word, he is able to copy not only the form of the sound and its pitch (or at least the higher-pitched sounds), but also the way your lips and tongue frame the word, and link the feeling you convey to the expression on your face. From an early age, your baby will be able to elicit meaning from your expression, and the lip and tongue movements and the sounds that you make. Talking to your baby, even if it is repeating a single word – 'Hello' – over and over again, will stimulate the learning process and build emotional links.

It is thought that babies have an inherent capacity to learn language and to identify certain sounds and sound combinations amid the constant babble (of the people and machines that make up their environment) that surrounds them. It could be compared to learning a foreign language, with its bewildering new vocabulary and rules of grammar, without taking lessons in it.

'Parentese'

Parental encouragement and stimulation are undoubtedly influential on the speed and ease with which your baby learns to talk. You may end up speaking in what is termed 'parentese' – short sentences said in an exaggerated tone of voice with long gaps between the phrases. Although this has a role to play in teaching your child language, try not to resort to this mode of speech all the time.

Language evolution

- **1–6 weeks – Non-verbal language**
  Crying, facial expressions, eye contact and movement of the hands and legs.

- **2–4 months – Cooing**
  Random, patternless vowel sound repeated whenever your baby feels content.

- **5 months – Random babbling**
  A wider variety of sounds made when your child has your attention.

- **6–9 months – Controlled babbling**
  'Pretend' speech, this can incorporate the same sounds used repeatedly.

- **10–11 months – Pre-speech**
  Uttered with a varied tone – individual words are not yet distinguishable.

- **12 months on – The first words!**
  And his vocabulary will continue to grow over the coming months.

Patterns and shapes

A newborn baby can recognize contrasts between light and dark and can see close objects. Even lying still in a pram or cot a baby will be investigating with his eyes the patterns and shapes around him – the edge of a pram cover, the bars of a cot, and the faces of people who come within range.

Recognizing shapes and colours

Amazing though it might seem, a baby can recognize different shapes at a very young age, although psychologists don't yet know exactly what young babies are actually seeing. Even so there is little doubt that a baby is capable of distinguishing between shapes such as a cross, a square, a circle and a triangle by staring at them, so it's a good idea to stimulate your baby by presenting him with a range of different-shaped objects. Don't worry about over-stimulating him: he is keen to get to grips with every new experience that comes his way.

Likewise, colour recognition occurs early on – and new babies even show a preference for one colour over another: they may stare for much longer at blue and green objects than they do at red ones. So choose bright, textured and shaped toys when selecting items for your baby to play with.

Is is these factors which may explain why the nondescript (to adult eyes) cardboard box that an expensive toy arrives in may be more successful than the toy itself: the box probably has bright colours, a lid and a smooth surface, which teach your child about colour, movement and texture and are an endless source of fascination.

Stimulating play

Hanging mobiles, particularly in a variety of shapes and colours, extend the environment for a very young baby. Put these within about 50 cm (20 in), but out of reach of investigative fingers as time progresses. When he does reach out, non-toxic plastic shapes of various colours provide excellent play value, as do rattles (particularly those stretched across the pushchair or pram within reach). Choose a variety of shapes, colours and sound effects to amuse your baby.

The aim, as at every stage of physical development, is to provide as diverse and stimulating play environment as possible to encourage the recognition of patterns and shapes. Through sight (the main sensory vehicle for learning in humans), sound and touch, learning progresses according to the variety of new near-matching experiences in the environment. Simply taking a young (and awake) baby for a walk or to the shops or to the park will change the environment, and thus the learning experience. Talking, listening to the various sounds and voices on the television and a variety of music will increase sound experience.

Stimulating your baby

From 0–12 months your child's development will involve phases of reaching, grasping, rolling over, sitting, crawling, and taking her first steps (the average age for walking is usually 15 months, although some children walk as early as eight months and as late as 18 months). At each phase, you will need to provide both a secure and stimulating environment in terms of sight, sound and touch.

Encouraging development

For babies of 0–12 months there are a wide variety of plastic shapes, plastic cups, rattles, squeaky toys, teething rings and play centres on the market that can help to stimulate your child's development.

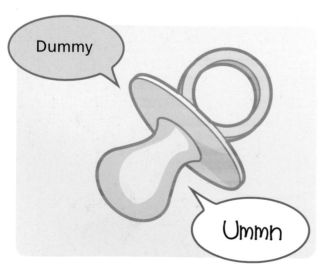

Dummy

Ummn

At about seven months, your baby will begin to recognize three-dimensional shapes in pictures, so she may show great interest in pictures of objects she knows already (bottle, chair, table, spoon, plate and so on). Showing pictures of objects and repeating the names for a short time each day can result in great intellectual strides being made later on – word meanings are the building blocks on which much abstract work is built.

An important step in encouraging your baby to communicate is to try to get her to point to, go to, or even say the word that names the object she wants (bottle, rattle, dummy, teddy...). As with all activities at this age, do not repeat the encouragement beyond the point where she is actively interested. On the other hand, if she is grunting and pointing at something it is time to try to get a definitive word. It is a question of persistence over a period of days, or even weeks, with a child who is, perhaps, nearing one year of age. Very quick-learning babies can, with much practice, copy spoken words at as young as a few weeks of age. At an older age, they can learn words with less practice, although they tend to be more focused on learning physical things, and investigating physically.

If you have a very physically active baby, you will have to try words, be patient, and wait. Words learned should only include those that your baby is very familiar with, and are also concrete (real-life objects), although words like 'yes' 'no', 'eat', 'drink', 'play' are also very valuable at this stage of development.

Songs and toys

Even very young babies will try to sway in time to music, sometimes making 'aah, aah' sounds and gurgling as they sway. Sound appreciation and differentiation in young babies are very well developed, and singing songs to your baby in your arms is another set of modifying experiences that can accelerate development. This is particularly applicable in the months leading up to her first birthday, although many children of this age seem consumed by the desire to crawl, walk, roll, climb, push and pull and the experience of merely sitting is of secondary interest.

Singing to your baby

There is a wide range of rhymes that can be sung with young babies, but small children equally enjoy almost endless repetition of just a few. Finger rhymes are much liked:

> Round and round the garden,
>   *(your fingers around her palm)*
> Like a teddy bear,
> One step, two steps,
>   *(fingers 'walk' up her arm)*
> Tick-a-ly under there.
>   *(tickle under her arm)*

This little piggy went to market, *(finger one)*
This little piggy stayed at home, *(finger two)*
This little piggy had roast beef, *(finger three)*
This little piggy had none, *(finger four)*
And this little piggy went *(finger five)*
Whee, whee, whee, all the way home.
    (fingers running up her arm to tickle)

Pat-a-cake, pat-a-cake, baker's man,
    (put the palms of your hand against hers)
Bake me a cake as fast as you can.
Pat it and prick it and mark it with B,
And put it in the oven for baby and me.
    (point to your baby and then to yourself)

Toys for 0–1 years

- Brightly coloured rattles
- Balls of a variety of colours and sizes
- Plastic and wooden bricks
- Plastic cups
- Picture cards
- Flannel and hardback books of pictures of everyday objects
- Play-centre
- Wooden spoons and saucepans
- Toy xylophone
- Boxes to put objects in and take out of

Baby on the move

3

1–2 Years

Naming objects

Although the period between one and two years is one of a great explosion of physical activity, your baby is still alert (for short periods) to more intellectual activities, either sitting on the floor, on your lap or up to a table. A combination of the following two methods will build up a knowledge of naming words, and also their use in forming sentences. Repetition is also important, and conscious efforts by parents to teach certain groups of words at a time ensures faster learning. Certain words will naturally arise more than others, but after these are known and repeated often, others can then be introduced.

How to approach naming objects

1 First, put the objects on the table and sit at the table with your child on your lap. Name the objects in turn, pointing at them as you say the word.

2 Next, introduce the objects into ordinary conversation. If, for example, your child wants a drink, ask him, 'Do you want the cup?', emphasizing the word cup. Or you can ask him to bring it to you, 'Bring me the cup', again emphasizing the word. Let him see the way your mouth works as you say the word, and let him hear the word clearly.

Try (as much as possible) to correct grunts and other 'own language' that he produces when asking for things. The sounds are appealing, but repeating them will delay him learning the real word. One toddler (nearly three years old) had built up a whole vocabulary of his own to ask for things, and his parents had responded by learning what he meant! In these circumstances, his learning of complete words had been held up for literally years.

Naming cards

These can be used to turn learning into an enjoyable game. Use three or four cards that have pictures of common objects on them. You could draw the pictures yourself or cut out pictures from magazines or print them out from the computer. Show the cards to your child and clearly pronounce the name of the object. Repeat this a few times then ask your child to name the objects on the cards in random order.

Action words and abstract words

These are extremely important for intellectual development, and are areas often neglected in pre-school learning. Action words can be built into sentences and can be drawn on naming cards, even as matchstick men.

You can ask: 'What is the man doing?'

First action words

sit walk lie run eat drink go come fall

These and certain abstract words can be built into short instruction sentences:

Short instruction sentences

Come here.	Sit down.	Sit still.
Lie down.	Go to sleep.	Get up.
Open the door.	Go in there.	Come out.
Shut the door.	Wave!	Clap!
Stop!	Throw!	Look!

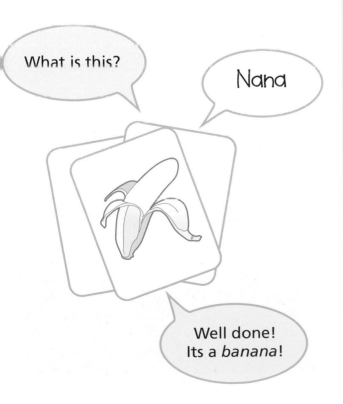

What is this?

Nana

Well done! Its a *banana*!

Two-word sentences with frequent repetition are learned best, later to be followed by three-word sentences, such as 'I want milk' or 'Give me teddy.'

A parent's input, clearly, is vital in extending near-matching and the development of memory. For recall, repetition is necessary, because of the difficulty of arranging 'pegging' with a young toddler. However, your child can understand more than he can say, and the more words he hears, the faster he is likely to learn.

Objects to name

On the face
eyes, mouth, ears, nose, hair, lips, teeth, eyebrows, eye lashes, cheeks

Parts of the body
arms, legs, head, feet, hands, fingers, toes, tummy, bottom, back, knees

Clothes
socks, shirt, skirt, dress, pants, coat, sweater, hat, scarf, gloves, shoes, boots

In the house
door, table, chair, plate, spoon, fork, knife, cup, potty, toilet, bath, bed, window, door

Food and drink
water, milk, biscuit, cake, sweets, cereal, potatoes, meat, cheese, bread, egg, sugar

Outside
car, house, bike, bus, tree, flower, bush, dog, cat, shop, road, bus, train, station

Size, shape and colour

Learning bricks are an invaluable tool when teaching your child the concepts of size, shape and colour. Play of this type ensures ease of learning and forms close links with more abstract work later on. Ease of learning is particularly important from 1–2 years to build your child's confidence in her abilities and fosters concentration.

Learning materials

You'll find a set of wooden bricks of different sizes, and other shapes of similar sizes (cuboids, prisms, cylinders, spheres, pyramids, cones) very useful. An ideal set would be:

• Ten cubes for counting

• Ten different-sized cubes for comparing sizes

• Several cuboids for comparing lengths

• Several shapes of similar size (cubes, prisms, cylinders) for sorting into shapes

• A number of similar size but different-coloured shapes for colour sorting (prisms in blue, yellow, green, red, for example).

Also seek out a set of plastic cups that fit into each other. The set should be of the same colour, and preferably cylindrical for ease of use. The plastic cups can be used for sorting activities and will create a foundation in memory for later learning of measurement and shape in maths.

Sorting activities

This is play for children, and it is play that is richly rewarding in a learning sense. Provided with the correct experiences, a child between the ages of 1–2 years and 2–3 years will develop at a faster rate than at any time in her life. Much of the development is physical, as she becomes more dextrous and more able to climb, run and jump; but, according to the level of input, pure intellectual ability is accelerated alongside such physical development.

Sorting and ordering for size
Different-sized bricks and cups can be arranged to illustrate size. Babies find ordering difficult, especially more than two or three.

Simply show your baby how to do this and leave her to play. Repetition over a period of weeks

and months will make the general idea of bigger and smaller clear. Eventually, it will be possible to point out 'small' or 'little' and 'big', to define the concept.

Towers are difficult for a child of this age to build. You can build a tower yourself and tell her that you are building a house or a church, or arrange the bricks horizontaly to build a train. The end and middle of the object can also be explained.

Note Ensure, however, that teaching new concepts does not coincide with a period such as the early weeks after learning to walk, when a child is naturally absorbed with getting around and investigating space. She will learn best sitting in her baby chair, in the bath, or on your lap, at such a time.

Sorting by shape
Place two of each shape in a small pile on a table. Show your baby how to sort into different groups of shapes (start with two different

shapes, and progress to three or four). Make sure that the colours of the shapes are the same.

This sorting activity can be extended to sorting plastic cups and saucers, knives and forks, socks and pants etc. Most children will find this difficult until they are nearly two (or even much later, at two or three years), but persist until your child grasps what you are asking her to do.

Sorting by colour
Use different-coloured bricks of the same shape. Start with two bricks of yellow and two of red. Show how to separate into colour groups. When she is competent at this, move on to three bricks of each colour. Later, move on to three colours (two bricks each). Naming colours is not necessary at this stage, unless a two-year-old is very quick at sorting activities, and has a good command of vocabulary.

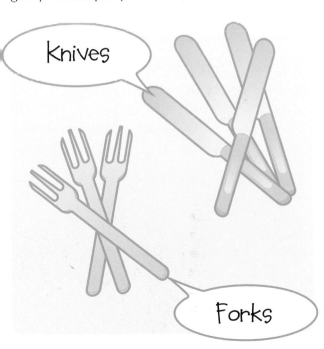

Sorting toys

Toys are associated with fun, so sorting them is a great way to get toddlers to learn. Spread a range of toys out in front of you and your child, then get him to sort them into different groups. You can sort them:

- By shape ('Let's put all the round toys together')

- By size ('Let's find all the big toys')

- By colour ('Let's put all the green toys together')

- By characteristic ('Let's find all the dolls/animals/toys with wheels')

You can even ask him how he thinks the toys should be arranged, and see what he comes up with.

Learning colours

Colour cards can be very useful for teaching the names of colours. Try this at about 18 months of age and see how your child gets on. Colours should be taught one at a time, usually after some sorting of colour has been successfully accomplished.

To make colour cards, cut some sticky paper of the colour you wish to teach and stick to a card. The card should be about double the size of a small envelope.

Show a particular colour card to your child and say, 'This is yellow'. Ask your child to find a similar-coloured object among the cubes and crayons, and elsewhere in the room. A couple of minutes a day over a period of weeks maybe needed to learn a single colour.

Fitting objects into space

With the beginning of crawling and walking comes the opportunity to extend the range of investigating. The in-built curiosity of a toddler leads him to search out cupboards and boxes and to climb stairs to explore other exciting places. This trying and testing of the environment is vital to further learning.

There are a variety of 'pegs in holes' toys that allow further exploration of shape. 'Posting boxes' are excellent for sorting shapes, but care must be taken to ensure that the ability of the toddler is equal to the difficulty level of the toy.

Providing tubs and boxes to empty and fill will extends your toddler's investigative potential as well as his knowledge of shape, and the relationships between size and weight, space and capacity.

Counting

Each of the following activities provides your child with good repetition, pegging for recall, and good opportunity for practice in understanding concepts and structuring memory that lead to easy links with later schoolwork. Counting up stairs is a good introduction to using the number line between the ages of five and seven (see page 92). Some number rhymes and songs will also be useful for later addition and subtraction practice.

Count with me – one, two, three

One, two, three

How to begin counting

- Using similar real objects (spoons, bricks, chairs, cars in the street, for example). Building towers of bricks and lines of bricks make the activity interesting and with an aim to achieve.

- Counting steps – the stairs up to bed or simply 'One, two, three' along the ground.

- Counting pictures of similar objects, either drawn or in a book.

- Counting fingers.

- Counting and number rhymes and songs.

Count first only to three with your child, even if it is fingers: 'One, two, three; one, two three…'

When your child is beginning to count well up to three, sing rhymes about the number three.

One, two, three,
baby and me,
(count on the fingers or toes)
Your tick-a-ly.
(touch your baby under the chin)

Then progress on to counting, using all methods, up to five, and follow eventually with rhymes such as:

One, two, three, four, five,
Once I caught a fish alive.

This Little Piggy Went to Market

Two Little Dicky Birds Sitting on a Wall

Round and Round the Garden like
a Teddy Bear

Exploring

Any toy which squeaks, talks, rings or makes another interesting sound will interest your child. Toys which move in a variety of ways, and those with a variety of shapes and colours will extend your child's play experience and encourage learning. However, the household, garden and park are also rich in things to investigate and learn. You and your child can discover a multitude of objects with different surfaces, shapes and consistencies.

Water play

Playing with water can link to concepts of capacity, fluidity and flotation later on. In the bath, at the sink, or in a bowl outside on a path or patio, let your child experiment with water and different-sized plastic cups. Show her how to fill up a big container from several small ones. Then let her play with these toys and other objects that float in the water.

Snow and ice

In the winter, show your child that snow, ice and frost melt into water. Leave an ice-cube in a cup and come back half an hour later. Ask, 'What's happened to the ice?' Show her how you make ice-cubes with orange juice for ice-lollies. This can be continued as she gets older

and understands your explanations better. Initially, it is difficult for many toddlers to link an ice-cube in a cup with the water left after a period of melting. What is happening only really becomes clear if they have the patience to sit and watch what happens.

Note The experience of a disappearing ice-cube is similar to the game of hiding a toy: toddlers do not have the experience in their memory to visualize what has happened when a hidden toy is moved elsewhere while they are not looking for a second. They feel it has 'vanished'. Explain and show what you did or what happened to enable your child to modify her knowledge of 'hidden' things. Most inadequacies in toddler thinking can be rectified if time is taken to fill in gaps in knowledge.

Sand tray

Sand in a shallow tray or box will provide further opportunities for investigatng solids and liquids. Sand has some of the properties of a liquid (it can be poured, and takes the shape of whatever it is put into), but there are no cohesive forces between the particles. Your child can learn about these properties using plastic cups or glasses. She can also hide things in sand, and when it is wet can build sandcastles and other shapes. Show her how to do these things, then leave her to play. Over a period of time try to teach at least a few word meanings relating to her play – empty, full, wet, dry, and so on.

Modelling clay and play-dough

These can also teach your child something about the properties of a solid which is very malleable and can be pushed and pulled into shapes. A two year old will need to be played with, and talked to about what you are doing with these materials. Descriptive words like 'soft', 'squishy' and 'smooth' are invaluable for building up the meaning of words.

Soft

Smooth

Squishy

Sand and dough

All of the following techniques can help toddlers learn about the properties of different materials through play.

Sand

- Provide a funnel, sieve or colander and let your child see what happens as she pours sand into them

- Offer your child cups, bowls, buckets and other containers to play with and to compare how much sand each contains

- After filling a small bag with sand, cut off the corner and let your child draw patterns with the stream of sand that flows out of it

- Make sandcastles, then ask your child to look around the garden, beach or surrounding area for suitable decorations: flowers, leaves, shells, lollipop sticks, and so on.

Play-dough

- Give your child some pastry cutters and show her how to cut out different shapes

- Roll out some play-dough into long sausage shapes, then make spirals, snakes and the outlines of a house with the long strips of dough

- Show her how to press coins, pebbles, shells and leaves into the dough and leave an impression behind

- Help her make a cast of her finger, hand or foot by pressing it firmly into a thick piece of dough.

Creative play

Creative activities provide an outlet for the expression of thoughts and feelings, as well as opportunities to try and test the boundaries of a toddler's world. Creative play gives your child the means to explore fantasies and stretch his imagination through games and role play.

Crayons

For this age group, short, chubby crayons and plenty of drawing paper are essential. In the first instance, show your child how to make squiggly lines on the paper, changing the colour of the crayons as you go. Then leave him to experiment for as long as he wishes.

Painting

Finger-painting is great for children of 1–2 years. Show your child how to dip a finger into the prepared finger paint, and make marks on the paper. Protection in the form of overalls for your child and newspapers or polythene to cover the table and floor is essential. Again, leave him to experiment, helping to replace paper and tidy up any mess when necessary.

Sticky-paper shapes

You can show a two-year-old how to stick small coloured shapes on to a large sheet of white or coloured paper or card. This, for some children, can be an all-absorbing activity for a long time. If your child finds this easy use large sheets of graph paper to extend the sticky-paper play – this provides a link to pattern, shape and symmetry learning later on. However if your child finds this activity too difficult leave it for a few months before re-introducing.

Note Make sure that the glue is non-toxic and suitable for children.

Role play

At 1–2 years, large dolls and large cars to sit them in, brushes, combs, and similar everyday items stimulate role play best. This play is generally solitary, but toddlers can be persuaded to play a little with older brothers and sisters.

Sadia, at 18 months, treated her doll like a little child, telling it off, sometimes in recognizable words and sometimes creating her own

language to express herself. Her sentiments were unmistakable, though:

'Bad!' she said. 'Sit down!'

There then followed dressing-up, and some completely unknown words. She brushed the 'baby's' hair and chattered to her with clear adult inflections. Not knowing the words was no bar to Sadia.

Smaller toys such as garages and houses are seen more as boxes in which to put things, but gradually children begin to use these also for role play. It is best to try a child with this type of toy from 18 months or two years onwards.

Acting, singing and dancing

Children coming up to two years of age love to dress up – by three, the first place they race to at the nursery school is often the dressing-up corner. Putting on their parent's shoes or boots or wearing an adult's hat and pretending to be big is a great joy. Children become ecstatic looking in the mirror at their appearance.

A good dressing-up box can stimulate role play considerably: straw hats, jackets, old dresses and shirts, handbags, jewellery, a variety of old adult shoes are all good items to include.

Provide a CD or cassette player so they can dance to children's songs, too. Most children move naturally in some way when they hear music: it may not be dancing as such, but they will probably sway their bodies and move in time to the music.

Music-making before two years of age is a rather haphazard thing, but do provide pots, pans, wooden spoons, a toy xylophone or a plastic trumpet. Your child will probably enjoy making actions while banging the instruments, too.

Musical games

To develop your child's language skills, try singing different songs in different ways and letting him watch the way your mouth moves – and then try to copy you himself. For instance, you might sing a few verses of This Old Man in a squeaky voice, a grumpy voice, a whisper, and so on:

This old man, he played one
He played knick-knack on my thumb
Knick-knack paddywhack, give your
    dog a bone
This old man came rolling home

This old man, he played two
He played knick-knack on my shoe …

This old man, he played three
He played knick-knack on my knee …

This old man, he played four
He played knick-knack on my door…

This old man, he played five
He played knick-knack on my hive…

This old man, he played six
He played knick-knack on my sticks…

Or you could sing This Old Man, Twinkle, Twinkle, Little Star or Hickory, Dickory, Dock and clap your child's hands together at the end of every line, to emphasize it and encourage his sense of rhythm.

Developing play

Play can help your child to begin to understand and solve problems. Toys that develop gross and fine motor skills, and those that stimulate intellectual growth are particularly important for children of 1–2 years. Activity centres, sorters, plastic cups and building bricks are all good purchases as they stimulate more than one aspect of development.

Problem-solving

- Creating scenarios involving incorrect placement or use of objects will entertain your child and encourage her to notice when

things aren't as they should be. As long as the appropriate use of clothes is first well established, putting shoes on her head (or your head), gloves on her feet, socks on her hand and so on will provoke fits of giggles at the silliness of it all. 'Eating' milk with a fork and brushing hair with the wrong end of a brush are other possibilities.

- Once your child has a good word and short-sentence knowledge, you can test her ability by producing picture cards showing objects with parts missing and ask her to tell you what's wrong with the picture.

- Try lining up three or four toys against the wall, ask her to close her eyes, and hide one. Ask, 'What has gone?' This is difficult for most two-year-olds, whose answer is usually to look for it to discover what has gone. With practice (after a few months), they get more proficient at remembering.

Animal hide-and-seek

Try hiding an animal toy and getting your child to look for it. After you have hidden the toy, say a rhyme such as:

Where is Koala Bear?
Where could he be?
Let's find him, quick as 1, 2, 3.

Then go and find the toy, pull it out and say, 'Look! Here's Koala Bear.' Next time, hide a different toy, but always say the rhyme (naming the correct animal) before looking for it. Then get your child to hide a toy herself. Say the rhyme with her, then let her find it.

Toys and activities

Toys

Bright-coloured activity quilts

Cot and pram mobiles

Activity centres

Soft alphabet blocks

Solid letters for the bath and play on the floor

Toy xylophone, trumpet or similar basic instruments

Balls in bright colours and patterns

Stacking rings that fit over a central core

Toy phones

Shape sorters

Plastic cups (to fit into one another)

Finger rhymes and songs

This Little Piggy Went to Market

Round and Round the Garden

Two Little Dicky Birds

Pat-a-cake, Pat-a-cake

Incy Wincy Spider

Diddle, Diddle Dumpling My Son John

Household objects

Saucepans, wooden spoons and the like, for making 'music'

Plastic cups, beakers, jugs for playing with in the bath

Cardboard boxes and things to put into them and take out (plastic cups, plates, spoons, forks and so on)

Any interesting objects for counting

Books

These can include cloth books and plastic bath books (your baby's attention is relatively focused in the bath), ABC books, nursery rhymes, and books with large, clear pictures of animals, transport, people and household objects. Read words and talk about the pictures. Say, 'Look, it's a plate' or 'It's a cat.'

The 'terrible twos' 2–3 Years

4

Talking

There will be no shortage of chit-chat at this stage, and the lines of enquiry are open! But you need to consider your answers quite carefully when you are responding to a very young child, usually by giving a word to define an experience. Talking is not just about naming objects – although this is important – but also about explaining feelings, behaviours and, in very simple terms, how things work and why certain things are dangerous. Not only that, but you need to show as much as possible in a practical or visual way, through drawings, actions, real-life objects, CDs and videos.

Learning power

Getting your child to create mental images by using the senses (sight, sound, touch, taste and smell) will strengthen her ability to match new with previous experiences, thereby helping her to make connections between things.

How to accelerate learning

- Continue to name everyday objects, especially when asked, and repeat the names as often as possible.

- Try to include more and more descriptive words – soft, hard, warm, cold, sad, happy, closed, open, poor, rich, dark, light, boiling, freezing, danger or dangerous.

- Try to explain every new word by showing pictures, diagrams or real-life objects.

- Make explanations short and easy to understand, using words that she knows.

- Initiate discussions as well as merely being the answerer of her questions. For instance, you could say 'That tree is big, isn't it?' If she says, 'Why is it big?' then you could say, 'It's been growing a long time. It's very old' and so on to engage her in conversation.

- Try to get your child to think beyond the surface of things, and to notice what is very close. Sitting with an information book full of pictures of animals, boats, trains, cars, people with different jobs, mountains, waterfalls, rivers, the seaside, the farm, the zoo or whatever is bound to provoke discussion that will widen her horizons.

- From time to time, correct her use of speech tenses and wrong words, or she will continue to use them incorrectly for months or years. Use short, good sentences with words that you feel will be understood.

- Encourage speech planning by reminding your child to give key details about the places, people and sequence of events when she recalls an incident. Ask questions as necessary to provoke her into giving you such details. She won't always be able to recall all of them, but the simple act of going through this process will be beneficial.

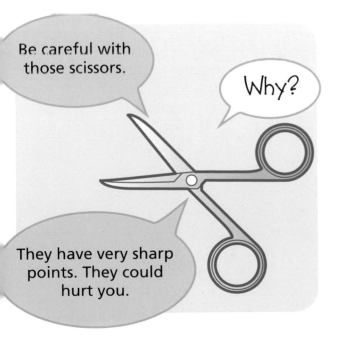

Be careful with those scissors.

Why?

They have very sharp points. They could hurt you.

Language development

Between the ages of two and three your child should show some or all of the following language skills:

- An ability to name the main parts of the body

- Testing out of different word combinations (although some of these may be incorrect or mispronounced)

- A keenness to ask questions (increasingly about what unfamiliar words mean) and to hear the answers from you

- A growing vocabulary of words, structured in short sentences

- The capacity to name everyday objects

- Recognition of her own name and age, and the ability to tell others what they are

- A love of bedtime stories (sometimes the same ones, read over and over again)

- Increasingly confident use of pronouns, such as 'I', 'me' and 'he', and of prepositions, such as 'in' and 'on'

- The ability to issue instructions to you

- An interest in other people's conversations, and in conversing with other children and with adults who are familiar to her

- The capacity to use language as an extension of play

- The ability to jump from one topic to another without becoming confused or diverted.

Games to provoke discussion

- I-Spy is an excellent game to start at this age. Choose a concrete object that you are certain he knows the word for, and define it using colour, shape and position: 'It's on the wall. It's red and it goes tick-tock.'

- Ask him to close his eyes while you make the sound of an object near him. You might try a whistle, keys, alarm clock, bell, bark or meow. Ask him to name the object and perhaps the name of the sound (although this is difficult for such young children).

- Repeat the second game but this time use objects that smell. Try an apple, orange, a favourite drink or chocolate. Ask your child to close his eyes, smell the object and tell you what it is.

- Repeat the game again and ask him to feel objects – a leaf, a watch, a spoon, a cup and so on.

Getting your child to create mental images through multi-sensory experience will strengthen the ability to near-match new experiences with memory.

It's round and light. If it bursts, it goes POP!

A balloon!

You can also help your child to understand what prepositions are by playing games with him: get him to stand beside the door, sit under the table, stand on the chair, jump over a book, put toys in the box, and so on. If he describes what he's doing using the same prepositions, this will reinforce them in his mind.

Body language

In addition to verbal language, body language begins to play a major role at this age and you can tell quite a lot about what your child is thinking by the way he stands, moves his hands and changes the expressions on his face.

- Good eye contact indicates that he is listening attentively to what you are saying and is largely in agreement

- Head thrown back and hands on hips are a sign of disagreement, anger or determination

- Scratching the top of his head or the back of his neck while he is talking to you is probably an indication of anxiety or embarrassment.

Reading to your child

Rhymes, riddles and short stories begin to fascinate at this age (coming up to three). Initially, the words themselves are not meaningful for a small child, so he will need to have many pictures to relate to as you read the story.

Books

Particularly relevant for this age are picture books with large, brightly coloured pictures with much to talk about in them. They might include short sentences for you to read, to continue the story or nursery rhyme, and the content should excite the imagination of a child. Fairy stories do this – 'Little Red Riding Hood', 'Snow White', 'The Three Little Pigs' are just some of the favourites – as do many nursery rhymes (especially when they can be sung as well). Nothing should be spared to capture your child's interest – if you have a keen listener at this age, it is most likely that you will have an avid reader later on, and consequently a child who is likely to succeed in a good proportion of the curriculum.

Linking nursery rhymes and fairy stories to videos and cartoon films will deepen interest and the enjoyment of books. At this age you can choose more challenging stories, rather than the simple, repetitive plots you were reading beforehand. Sit next to him as you read the book and follow the words with your fingers as he watches. Afterwards, ask whether he liked the story and why (or why not), and who the main characters were.

Don't forget to explain difficult words to him as you read – or he may ask you what a particular word signifies. It can be difficult to explain words whose meaning we take for granted, but try to be patient, so that he can associate the words he hears you using with an idea that has some meaning for him.

Rhymes, songs and poetry

Read anything that has rhythm, particularly if it is short and snappy. Read with feeling, and even actions, because toddlers of this age are learning more from inflections and related movements than they are from the actual storyline. Try to deepen the voice for a giant, cackle for a witch, and so on. At the end of this chapter is a list of much-loved songs and nursery rhymes.

Labels

There are words all around children in the home (on food packaging and labels, on letters and magazines, on boxes and containers) and in the wider world (on signposts, shop fronts and in supermarkets) and reading doesn't necessarily have to mean books. You can even label everyday items in the house so that your child becomes used to associating particular words with particular objects. Try turning this into a game by asking your child to spot particular labels in the supermarket or on street signs.

Pre-reading

Some children have been taught to read at a very young age – indeed one boy at ten months, several at two years, many at three years of age. However, many do not (for one reason or another) begin to read until they are four or five. Very young readers who are, without exception, fast learners in all subjects, retain great enjoyment in reading throughout life. One boy, an intense reader as a toddler, got top university entrance grades at 17 in English and drama, and also passed the university entrance exam in maths as a small boy.

Using picture cards

It is worth, therefore, trying a toddler with a set of picture cards, using them in a play way. Well-known objects can be drawn on card (or cutouts pasted on) and the word written large and clear in lower-case letters below or above the picture.

In a reading session, you can take the cards out, point to both picture and word and say the name. Do not labour over this. Sometimes, simply asking, 'What's this?' will get an immediate response. Your child is, of course, naming the object in the picture. The word is not being focused on, but, with time, as your finger continually points to both word and picture together, the association between the written word and the concrete object will develop. At some point, covering up the picture will elicit an immediate response with the saying of the word. You will know if she does not recognize the word, because she will try to raise your hand to look at the picture. The whole process must be managed with parental diplomacy so that no trace of a sense of failure develops in your child.

Some books approach the word-and-picture association system extremely well and allot a full page to each picture with its associated word. This isolation of a concept, one thing to concentrate on at a time, makes matching easier. Large letters also help in this respect.

Further counting

Extend counting of a variety of real objects, and pictures, according to your child's progress, up to five, and then ten.

Counting objects

Buttons, coins, fingers, pencils, cakes, matchsticks, spoons, marbles and teddies are examples of concrete objects that can be used for counting exercises. Ask your child to count steps on ladders, stairs and pathways. Try putting little pictures on steps to create an idiosyncratic image. There can be pictures of cars, men, trees, dogs, cats, stars, crosses, dots, circles...the possibilities are endless.

Using an abacus

Start with an abacus with big 'bands' for counting up to five. Using an abacus also helps with colour-sorting. When your child can count well up to ten, invest in a 10 x 10 abacus for both the present and the future.

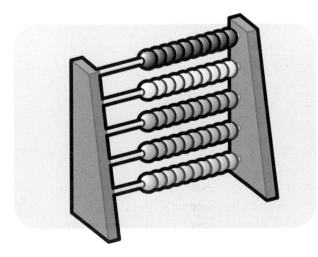

One, two, three ...

Counting rhymes

These can be extended to keep up with your child's knowledge.

One, two, buckle my shoe,
Three, four, knock at the door,
Five, six, pick up sticks,
Seven, eight, lay them straight,
Nine, ten, a big fat hen.
(use actions and sounds to act out this rhyme)

One man went to mow,
Went to mow a meadow,
One man and his dog,
Went to mow a meadow.
Two men went to mow, etc.
(you could also use dolls, teddies, toy men, etc.)

One big teddy, sitting on the chair,
One big teddy, sitting on the chair,
If one more teddy should climb upon
   the chair,
There'd be two big teddies sitting on
   the chair.
Two big teddies, sitting on the chair...
*(sing to the tune of 'Ten Green Bottles',
   and use teddy bears and fingers to
   emphasize the numbers)*

Shapes

Your child will already be using a variety of shaped bricks to play and build things with, even if haphazardly. Now he's reached the stage where he can build much better and much higher you can begin introducing further shape learning.

Learning shapes

The learning of shapes moves from the general to the specific at 2–3 years – the idea of 'squarey' (square, rectangle, cube, window) will become entrenched in memory at some point, so words like 'square' are key ones, as is 'triangle' and 'circle' (or 'round'). You can ask your child to pick out square or square-like shapes in the environment, as well as triangle shapes, and round ones. These concepts, at this stage, are approximations and examples are:

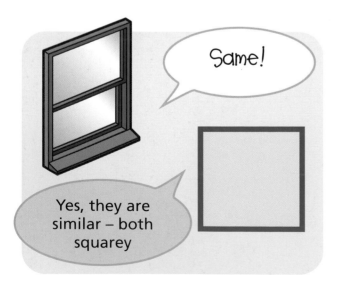

Same!

Yes, they are similar – both squarey

Sorting the shopping

Putting away the supermarket shopping is a good way to get your child used to different-shaped objects. Ask him to help you put your purchases in your kitchen cupboards and he'll learn how to put (round or square) biscuit packets together, (roundy) tins in one cupboard and (squarey) cereal packets in another. He might even come across (triangley) candles or wedges of cheese. All of this subtly reinforces the message you are trying to get across.

square ('squarey')
square, rectangle, cube, cuboid, box, window, bus, door, TV

triangle ('triangley')
triangular prism, pyramid, cone (with some 'roundiness')

round ('roundy')
circle, sphere, ball, moon, sun, wheel

Specific names can be built on to these three groups later.

From time to time you can point out words related to shape such as:

over, under
tall, small
wide, narrow
sharp, round
edge, surface

Sorting and matching

By making a game of the following every-day activities you can encourage your child's development. As forms of problem-solving these activities are invaluable while being entertaining enough to maintain your child's interest.

Sorting and matching activities

- Ask your child to sort through a pile of socks and try to match the pairs.

- Show him how to sort washing into several piles – say, towels, shirts and underwear.

- Use words from cards from children's card games to match up similar things.

- Ask your child to sort plastic cutlery into separate piles. Start with small numbers of each and just two kinds, say knives and forks. Once he's got the hang of it, extend to larger numbers of each and introduce spoons.

- As with cutlery, do the same with plastic crockery (plates and saucers; then plates, saucers and cups), building up the level of difficulty as he masters each task, and taking the lead from your child.

- Ask your child to tidy up his toys, sorting them into piles as he goes – 'Dolls here, cars here, balls here.' Help him as much as he needs.

- Pairing is more difficult, but most children learn very quickly. Get him to pair plasic knives with forks, cups with saucers, etc. You will have to show him how, because words can be misunderstood at this age.

- Once sorting and pairing has been grasped, ask him to lay a place at the table.

Matching colours

Colour cards can be made by sticking coloured sticky paper over old playing cards. Start with bright, unambiguous colours: blue, green, red, yellow, orange, purple, white, black. As with other things, one colour should be tackled at a time. Point out similar colours in the room or outside, and play 'I-Spy colours' to add to the interest. You can also encourage him to draw or paint in a particular colour.

I spy with my little eye something YELLOW!

Ball!

Investigating

Children of this age have a great desire to 'find out', and your input is guiding a small proportion of your child's time into activity that builds towards and links with school investigations. It builds knowledge of strategies, patterns of discussing and problem-solving – adding to the development of the thinking process, although obviously at a rudimentary level.

The coin sinks

tops will sink when filled with water; and show her that plastic modelling clay will float if it is thinned out and boat-shaped.

Heavier and lighter

- Buy a weighing balance.
- Show your child how to find out which of her toys is the heavier. Say, 'This toy is heavier

The plastic duck floats

The car is heavier

Floating and sinking

She can now discover for herself the sort of things that will float and sink. Provide a range of objects – plastic cups, coins, metal toys, matchsticks, plastic modelling clay, plastic and metal bottle tops, dolls, marbles – and let her decide. You can point out that the metal bottle than that toy.' The end going down is associated with heavier, and the visual evidence makes the principle easier to understand and match into memory.

- You can help her to line up her toys from the lightest to the heaviest.

Air

Demonstrate that air has pressure by showing her that bubbles can be made when you blow through a straw into water or a drink. Show her that she can feel the air on her face when you blow towards her, and her hair is ruffled. She can also blow to make small waves on a bowl of water or in the bath. Relate blowing like this to the wind blowing the leaves on the trees, and blowing her hair into disarray.

All the senses

Continue hearing, smelling, touching and tasting activities with eyes closed (see page 46). Ask your child to try to describe what she is recognizing through her sense, so extending vocabulary and descriptive powers. Help out as she does so, using words like:

    smell, taste, touch

    push, pull, hold, pick

    sharp, soft, hard

    hear, loud, quiet

    sweet, horrible, nice,

Investigating fruits and vegetables
Show your child potatoes, carrots, cabbage, sprouts, onions, apples, oranges, bananas, pears, peaches and any other fruit and vegetables. Let her taste them to see which tastes the best. Cut an apple in half to show the pips. Open up a plum or peach to show the stone.

Looking in the mirror
Show your child her eyes, nose and ears in the mirror. See if she can see the colour of her eyes.

Parts of the body
Teach your child the names of some parts of the head and body, and what they are for.

    eyes – to see

    ears – to hear

    mouth – to eat

    nose – to breathe and smell

    hair – to protect the head

    hands – to touch and to hold with

    feet – to walk with

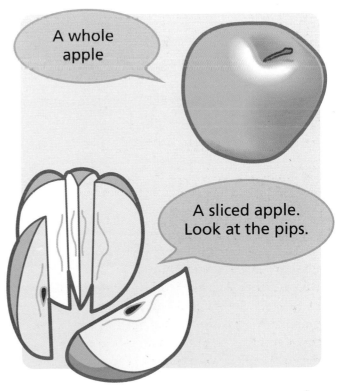

A whole apple

A sliced apple. Look at the pips.

Creative activities

At 2–3 years your child's play will naturally become more creative and imaginative. He will begin to use a paintbrush and thinner crayons, and will be more interested in drawing and painting shapes rather than the haphazard squiggle lines of the earlier years. There is more pretend play at this stage, so dressing-up boxes (with old clothes, shoes, hats) become more used.

Drawing and painting

Drawing skills can be developed with the use of coloured pencils and thin crayons. Show your child how to hold a pencil (fine motor skills allow this by about two and a half years) and how to draw horizontal, vertical and oblique lines and arcs. See if he can copy a large circle (copying should begin at about this age).

As well as teaching him to use a thick-bristled paintbrush you could also try potato printing. Cut a potato in half and cut out a simple design in the cut surface. He can then dip it into a saucer of paint and stamp a pattern on to paper. Once this is mastered try other objects and investigate the different shapes.

Cutting with scissors

By the time he is three years old, your child will usually be capable of making cuts in paper using blunt-ended scissors. Help him to cut through things – he will not be able to cut round things yet.

Acting, music and dancing

After reading a story, ask your child to act out the part of a character. Get your child to dance to children's songs or pop music. He may also want to sing along with the songs.

String and paper crafts

Try the following activities with your child as variations on the painting and cutting activities suggested above:

- Dip a piece of string into some paint, then ask your child to pull the string across a piece of paper to make a pattern or a wiggly snake.

- Fold a piece of paper in half, then open it out and let your child paint on one half of the paper. Refold it and press the paper smooth to spread the paint, then let your child open it up and see what kind of pattern he has created.

- Fold another piece of paper in half and help him to cut out simple shapes – a V, for instance – along the fold. Then get him to open up the paper and admire his cut-out design.

Toys and activities

Toys

Very popular from two and a half years on are small play people and small-scale, real-life buildings such as farms, zoos, vehicles, garages and train sets. There are excellent construction sets of large-scale plastic bricks for the slightly older child.

Let's pretend kits include outfits for nurse, doctor, policeman/woman, firefighter; sit and drive vehicles with steering wheel; house sets with pretend cookers, fridges, food, dinner sets, irons, tea sets, tables, chairs, play houses.

Games

Picture cards and visually-interesting jigsaw puzzles are the basis for structured games at 2–3 years. Try introducing the following:

Picture dominoes
Snap
Happy Families
Picture pairs and matching cards
Jigsaw puzzles of four to six pieces

Songs and nursery rhymes

Three Blind Mice

Jack and Jill

Oranges and Lemons

Pop! Goes the Weasel

See-saw, Margery Daw

Here We Go Round the Mulberry Bush

Old MacDonald Had a Farm

If You're Happy and You Know It Clap Your Hands

Books

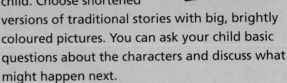

Start reading fairy stories with plot structures to your child. Choose shortened versions of traditional stories with big, brightly coloured pictures. You can ask your child basic questions about the characters and discuss what might happen next.

Further activities

- See if he can draw a circle and a cross on paper. You may need to draw the shapes first and ask him to copy.

- Try him with the names of a range of household objects. Ask, 'What is this called?' and 'What is it used for?'.

- See if he knows some action words – you can demonstrate walk, run, jump, sit, and so on and ask him to name the action.

- Try him with some abstract words: 'Tell me what is cold' (hot, hard, soft, big, little, fat, thin).

- Ask him to build a tower of wooden bricks.

- Try him with a six-piece jigsaw.

- Ask him to build a bridge with wooden bricks.

- Ask him some colours. 'What colour is this?' Try yellow, red or whatever you have taught him. Alternatively, ask 'Which one is red?'

- Ask him to sort some spoons from forks or cubes from spheres (or similar alternatives).

- Try dipping vegetables, hard fruit, nutshells, stones and bottle tops into a saucer of paint to make patterns on paper.

Springboard age 3–4 Years

5

Learning principles

At 3–4 years you and your child can begin to pursue activities closely allied to future academic work. The learning principles explained in earlier chapters must continue to be closely followed, otherwise gaps will appear in your child's memory, and important stepping stones will be lost.

Learning styles

The successful learning of maths depends on teaching counting well at the beginning – counting is the foundation concept that must be learned before the subject can be progressed, as illustrated below. Reading, on the other hand, has no particular starting point, yet all the concepts that contribute to reading must be learned for reading to be sucessful.

Learning time

Setting aside times in the day for some structural learning is important – your child will see the time as a natural part of every day, and new learning can be easily consolidated (too long between learning periods diminishes recall).

No longer than half an hour at a time is usually advised, and this should include several activities to cover the main learning areas. Rewards for effort are important, as is a relaxed, non-oppressive attitude. Try dividing the activities as follows:

5 mins	Drawing/copying letters
5 mins	Learning colours from cards/real life
5 mins	Counting
5 mins	Word meanings
5 mins	Alphabet letter sounds
5 mins	Story/talking about things/riddles/rhymes

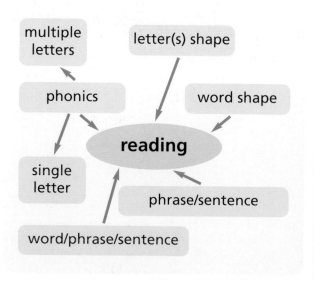

Length, weight and volume

Science is all about questioning, and children of this age are naturally observant and want to know why things happen – even if they don't necessarily comprehend the answers. Length, weight and volume are good areas to start with, as they will satisfy your child's curiosity and her longing to understand.

Length

There are two aspects of length that you can teach: comparison of lengths, and measuring. Use straws or lengths of string to explain 'long', 'longer' and 'longest', then 'short', 'shorter', 'shortest'. This also shows that you need more than two for the superlative (-est).

For measuring, units are not important at first. Let her measure using strides, foot-length or hand-spans. You could also try making a cardboard metre stick.

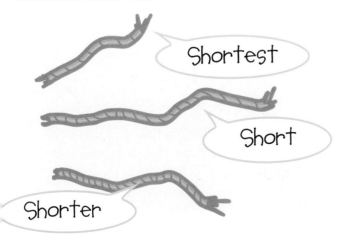

Shortest

Short

Shorter

Weight

Potatoes are invaluable kitchen assets for comparing weight and finding which is big (heavy), bigger (heavier), and biggest (heaviest) as they come in so many different shapes and sizes. Set out three potatoes of varying sizes and ask your child to compare them. She will need to handle them quite thoroughly at this stage to determine which is the lightest and which is the heaviest.

Weighing should be by comparison only at ages 3–4 – the teaching of weight units comes later. Once your child has learned how to compare objects of the same type she can begin to compare the weights of toys, first estimating by comparing weights and then moving on to using kitchen scales.

Volume

To demonstrate comparative volumes, take three identical plastic cups and fill each with different amounts of water. Explain that the cup holding the most amount of water is holding the greatest volume, while its capacity remains the same as the other cups.

'How much?' is a difficult question when talking about volumes and capacities, mainly because of a liquid's ability to adapt to the shape of a container. Try using two different-sized containers and ask, 'Which holds most water?' Let your child pour water from one to the other to find out. This is such a difficult concept that water play-time should involve no more capacity play than this at three years of age.

Maths

Such is the love of counting among three-year-olds, it is a wonder that so many end up with a hatred of maths at 11 years old. The fault lies not in an inability to relate the abstract to real life – number work can have a magic and fascination all of its own – but is often because of some relentless need to press on with new concepts, before necessary prerequisites are properly understood.

Counting

Three-year-olds are happy to count everything. Mark tells me on a bus trip into town, 'There's 12 cows in that field.' Then later, 'There's 15 lamp-posts, and 6 cars, and 4 men...' and so on, until he's got me silently counting everything that appears on the horizon, too. Some children 'stick' at numbers like 13 or 14 and 15 or 16, and then at 20 and 30. This seems to be due to parental boredom after getting things going up to a particular number, but you will need to persist all the way up to 100, and even beyond.

Numbers and number matching

Actual numbers should not be introduced until counting is well under way, and preferably when your child can write letters fairly well. Making number cards (see above) is very useful.

Cards for number matching should have the number on one side and markers on the other side. Use two sets of such cards (1 to 5), turn one set upside down and ask your child to match numbers to markers.

Patterns in the counting of numbers

When your child knows the counting numbers well, you can investigate patterns, first in the 1 to 10 series, then up to 20. Mind links (number bonds) developed here are useful in school when doing shopping sums, and generally in multiplication, division and fractions.

A counting table (see page 61) of numbers can identify many patterns. You could write up the numbers 1–10 or 1–20 on a large piece of card, and mark significant numbers in different colours or by circling them.

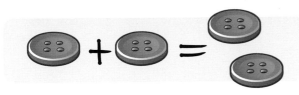

Adding

Using wooden bricks and building upwards is probably the best way to teach adding. It relates to the later idea of negative numbers, and the thermometer (which shows the concept of below zero). So, adding is going up, subtraction is going down.

Simon's difficulty, like many three-year-olds, is his impatience to rush on, thus losing the concept. In his mind is the fact that he knows how to build a big tower now, and looks forward to the destruction of the edifice.

Sums are often presented horizontally in textbooks and at school, so the use of buttons, sweets or counters in a row can provide an extra link to adding.

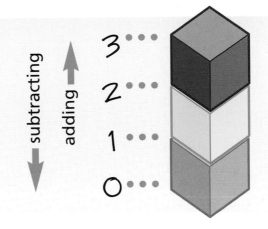

Counting with coins

One of the most endearing characteristics of three-year-olds is their naivety about money.

'Look, I'm rich,' says Fatima, showing me a bag full of coins, in total barely enough to buy a packet of sweets. When she and I set about counting it, she counts every coin as one unit, whatever its value.

Initially, then, you should use only one-unit coins to cement the counting. When it comes to using two-unit coins, tap twice on the coin to show that you count twice on it. Children learn early on that handing over money is associated with getting something in return, whether it's at the supermarket, the department store, or in a cash or drinks machine. You can play a basic 'trading' game using circles of paper cut out as money, counting each circle as one unit. If he wants to play with his favourite train, for instance, he has to trade for this by giving you one unit of money.

Even numbers are green. Odd numbers are red.

Reading

Encouraging a love of books in your child is so important that it needs to be the number one priority on your teaching list. It is an area about which many parents are very thoughtful and conscientious. They realize that a story read to their child sitting on their lap, or at bedtime, does cement a love of reading. If, later on, those same children come to me and say, 'Books are boring', then I know that books are lacking, not the children's desire to read.

Reading with your child

There are certain authors and books that always hold the attention of child readers – especially books by Roald Dahl and Enid Blyton's Famous Five series.

At three years what a child needs in a story is threefold:

1 A picture page, to talk about.

2 A few words with each picture.

3 Lively characterization, plenty of action, humour and some mystery.

Many fairy tales have these elements, although they can be rather gruesome (some children have dreams about witches and giants).

When reading stories to your child, dispense with your inhibitions, and enact the role of the giant or the witch. With every three-year-old I read to, after the second or third reading, she is doing the voices and the actions ahead of me!

Books need not be expensive. You can find story books, picture books, information books, ABC books of every shape, size and type at garage sales, local fairs, second-hand bookshops and school functions as well as libraries and main retail outlets.

Rhymes and jingles

Rhymes and jingles probably alert more pre-schoolers to the joys of reading than any other material. There are books galore of these rhymes, such as Hot Cross Buns, Pop! Goes the Weasel, Jimmy Crack Corn and The Wheels on the Bus Go Round and Round.

Rhyme and rhythm make for both greater memorability and greater enjoyment, and with a picture and actions, like clapping, create a truly multi-sensory mental image. Even the alphabet is sung and clapped out rhythmically in most early classes. A sense of rhythm can be encouraged by using 'shakers' (you could just use a matchbox half-filled with dead matches) or 'drums' (a wooden spoon on upturned ice-cream containers).

Key words (Group 1)

I, he, she, it, a, the, this, that, and, in, to, of, is, was

Teaching your child to read

There comes a point when your child will surprise you by repeating words from the pre-reading activities, such as a word in an alphabet book (such as 'apple'). When this happens varies a lot. With John, he did it at ten months of age while he was sitting up in his pram. Mark started repeating words at two and a half years, James at three and a half, and Michael at four.

From this point, you can choose one of several starting points: the phonic alphabet, look and say words (key words), or short sentences ('Here is Spot.'). Ultimately, all reading elements have to be covered.

The adoption of a structured building system in reading is important when teaching very young children, and has astonishingly good results in teaching older children whose reading lags behind. The mind builds in a very routine, sequential way, so it is wise to teach your child in the way the mind demands.

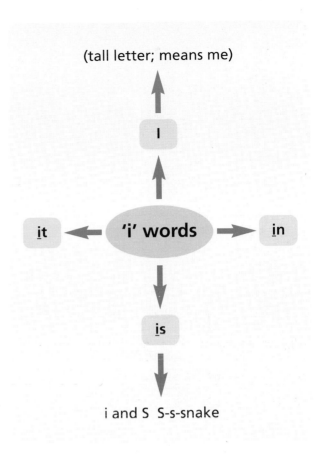

(tall letter; means me)

I

it ← 'i' words → in

is

i and S S-s-snake

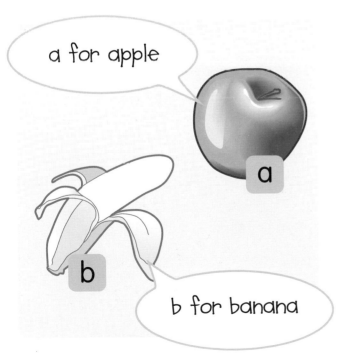

a for apple

a

b

b for banana

Letter shapes and sounds

Emphasize a concrete connection to letters. You can make a game of finding words with a 'short a' (as in 'rat', not 'rate' or 'rather'), or a short 'b' and so on. Initially, this is hard for a three-year-old, but improvement is surprisingly fast.

Word shapes and sounds

Learning words, especially concrete words, by association with a picture or real-life object is probably the best way to start reading. In addition, introduce some key words. Key words are words that occur most frequently in text and are usually abstract words (see box on page 62). Abstract words are more difficult to attach to a clear visual 'peg', so great repetition of these helps accelerate the reading process.

Reading games

Any of the following exercises will encourage familiarity with words and a keenness to experiment with them:

- Hunting for particular letters (say, a capital L if your child's name is Leanne) on food packaging

- Finding a favourite brand of biscuit or cake at the supermarket

- Looking for often-repeated words, such as 'and' or 'the', in books

- Naming flowers, animals or birds seen in the countryside

- Looking for different letters (or even words) in car number plates

- Playing 'I-Spy'

- Making up silly-sounding rhymes: the sillier, the better.

Tracing the key words (see page 62) in the air or in a sand tray, or making the words for your child using modelling clay or play-dough, help to create the more complete mental picture.

Books from which to teach reading need to have large, clear type and one short sentence per page, with interesting colourful pictures: for example, 'I see a bus', with a picture of a bus on the page. The picture-with-sentence format is often used as a 'peg' to hang a sentence on for easy recall.

Blends

Learning phonics certainly does not provide the complete answer to word-building but it is an important part of it. Gloria, at nearly four, stumbles over word-building because she reads 'th' as 't'. Also, 'they' includes not only 'th' but 'ey', which reads as 'ay'. 'They' happens to occur in the second group of key words, so is common in text and is learned fairly quickly by word shape – sound recognition. However, many words need building from scratch at the beginning of reading. This process is explained more fully in the next two chapters.

Opposites

It is the meanings of words that are important, as well as sounds and forms. Opposites create a clear mind image of meaning.

Opposites cards can be made for matching. Put six cards – three pairs of matching opposites – in a pile and ask your child to sort them. It usually takes several sessions before the idea sinks in. Children who are approaching four years are also far more adept than those just three. (If your child finds this too difficult, do the game first using pairs of identical cards at a time for matching.)

Problem-solving

Problem-solving ability can be developed from a young age. This is different from puzzle-solving (included later), which is often shape-matching and largely manipulative. As described in previous chapters you can create a problem with one answer to help your child learn the concept, then move on to multiple answers once he has grasped the idea.

Creating problems for your child to solve

Create a problem with only one answer:

> **Me** 'There is something yellow in this room, and it's nice to eat.'
> **Mark** 'Banana, but you got to take the skin off.'

What's yellow and nice to eat?

Banana!

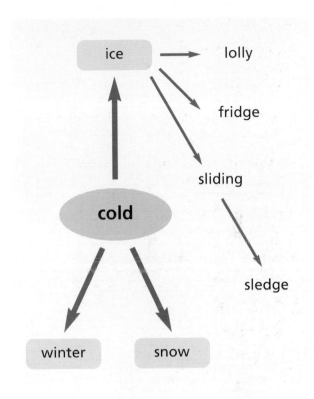

Alternatively, a problem can have a creative element, and have several answers:

> **Me** 'What is cold, Sadia?'
> **Sadia** 'I got to put my coat on.'
> **Me** 'Yes, but what is cold when you touch it?' (demonstrating – touching the table with a finger)
> **Sadia** 'Lolly. I got it yesterday. Mother said I mustn't run in the road…'

This is an area that should be developed, using elements that you know your child has in his memory, forging links between knowledge groups.

Make problems of word meanings and their opposites, especially where it leads to humour. Children often find 'What is wrong?' pictures fascinating and funny.

Squeals of delight came from Hannah when her knowledge of reality was tested:

1 'Where do cars sleep at night?'

2 'I sleep on the pavement every night.'

3 *Me* 'You're a giant. I'm a little wiggly worm.'
Hannah 'Don't be silly. You're big. I'm little.'
Me (I snuggle down low in my armchair)
   'You're silly. Look. I'm much littler than you.' *(Screams of laughter from Hannah.)*

4 'Where do you live, in a castle? Are you the King?'

However, asking, 'Does Father use a key to wind up the car every morning?' leads often to serious thought, since three-year-olds are very uncertain of how things really work.

Riddles

These are another way of extending your child's thinking, although one can easily misread a small child's conceptual thinking:

> *Me* 'What is thin, wriggly, and lives in the ground?'
> *Michael* 'Elephants.' *(very definitely)* 'They got wiggly trunks.' *(Of course, he does not distinguish between 'in' and 'on'.)*

Make some riddle cards. On one side draw or stick a picture. On the other side write a short description for you to read out. Lay the cards picture-face down, and read them out, turning them over when she gets it right.

Puzzles and card games

Manipulative ability, speed of matching, and spatial thinking are developed by jigsaws (including floor puzzles), and simple card games like snap, Happy Families and others.

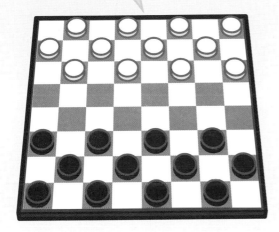

Move diagonally, one square at a time

Counting games

Ludo, draughts, Snakes and Ladders and hopscotch extend basic counting, although in Snakes and Ladders there is an element of addition that causes three-year-old children some difficulty.

Draughts is a good trainer of memorizing and recall – as is chess, which John learned well at three and a half. Using darts with 'suckers' and boards with numbers up to only ten is useful to make addition more meaningful, but only when your child has learned symbol addition well.

Construction toys

The three-dimensional element of matching is a natural extension of the young toddler's brick-building – there are several varieties of plastic, wooden and, later, metal construction toys involving a variety of shapes that test and encourage creativity and problem-solving.

DIY construction

As well as buying construction kits from shops, you can make many toys at home using materials that you probably already have to hand. Try the following suggestions:

- Get an empty plastic bottle and part-fill it with shells, buttons, coloured pasta, or any other small items. Pierce a hole in the lid, pull a knotted piece of string through the hole, and your child has a ready-made pull-along toy. You could even make wheels by cutting out four small circles of cardboard, piercing central holes in them, and then threading two wooden skewers through one side of the bottle and out the other side, before positioning the wheels on the outside of the skewers.

- Make a place setting from boxes, card and paper. Paint postcards or the edges of cereal boxes black for roads or railway tracks, then add markings in white paint or nail polish. Make houses and shops from boxes and matchboxes; parks and lawns from pieces of cardboard painted green; and trees from toilet-roll holders with pieces of green paper stuck in the top as branches and leaves. Then your child can simply add toy cars, trains or pipe-cleaner people and animals, depending on whether her chosen setting is a town, railway station or farm.

Investigations and activities

Simple investigations based on science and nature will stimulate a child of 3–4 years to think for himself and explore the rules that give order to his environment. Some ideas for fun and educational investigations are given below but if you wish to develop this further there are hundreds of excellent investigations books on the market you can work through with your child.

Investigation ideas

Here are a few ideas for investigations you can set up with your child. Some are continuations from the previous chapter and others are new ideas.

- **Growing mustard and cress** – try placing mustard or cress seeds in an egg shell with a piece of damp cotton wool and watch your child's delight as the seeds begin to shoot.

- **Floating and sinking** – fill a bowl with water and try various objects to see if they float or sink. Coins, stones, plastic cups and small sticks are all good objects to start with.

- **Light and heavy** – investigate whether heavy objects fall to the ground faster than lighter objects and how shape affects the fall rate. Try pieces of paper, balls, cotton wool and a small stone. See what happens when the piece of paper is screwed up.

- **Paper planes** – try making paper planes out of brightly coloured or patterned paper and watch them fly. Your child will love this. You can also try flying the planes outside on a windy day.

- **Collecting leaves** – collect various types of leaves from a garden or park and ask your child to group them according to shape and size. Look at how the shapes and colours vary.

- **Freezing and melting** – fill an ice-cube tray with water and leave in the freezer until frozen. Ask your child to compare water with ice and tell you the differences. You can then leave the ice-cubes to melt and time how long this takes.

- **Magnets** – ask your child to use a magnet to pick up paperclips or hair grips. Try holding two magnets together to see how they either attract or repel each other.

- **Fruits and vegetables** – gather a selection of different-shaped fruits and vegetables (e.g. banana, carrot, pineapple, onion). Encourage your child to feel the different shapes and textures and describe them to you. You could also cut fruits in half to look at the seeds.

Look what happens to the paper clips!

Toys and activities

At 3–4 years your child will have more control over his direction in drawing. This will eventually lead to the beginnings of writing and the following toys and activities can help with this.

Toys

Writing desk

Large floor jigsaw puzzles

Alphabet floor puzzles

Tracing paper

Blackboard and easel

Stencils and templates

Talking story books

Jigsaw puzzles

Scissors

Bicycles and pedal cars

Games

Marbles

Hopscotch

Matching pairs games

I-Spy

Dominoes

Snap

Songs

Hickory, Dickory Dock

Twinkle, Twinkle Little Star

It's Raining, It's Pouring

The Bear Walked Over the Mountain

One Finger, One Thumb, Keep Moving

Heads and Shoulders, Knees and Toes

The Animals Went in Two by Two

How Much is That Doggy in the Window?

We All Live in a Yellow Submarine

Old MacDonald Had a Farm

Counting songs

All good children, count together

One – two – three – four – five

One, Two, Buckle My Shoe

Ten Green Bottles

Books

Continue reading rhymes, fairy stories and picture books – by 3–4 years your child will have developed strong favourites. He will also love made-up stories about people and places he is familiar with. There is a wealth of books to read, with good, colourful pictures and interesting stories.

Creative play

The importance of play, both directed and undirected, cannot be overestimated. Through such activities the bounds of behaviour can be tested without fear of harm (crashing a toy car, for instance), role play can be acted out and links are forged between unrelated areas of knowledge. Creative play at this age can link to creative school activities, and can also develop rudimentary lateral thinking, and divergent (multi-answer) problem-solving.

Toys

Toys for creative play should include real-life toys (dolls, cars, trains, small people, police station, fire station, nurse's set, dressing-up clothes and the like). For imaginative play, almost anything goes – Roger used stones and twigs from the garden, plastic bricks, and bits of modelling clay to create a world far removed from reality, including sound effects of startling originality. Most children will love make-believe and should be encouraged to be creative.

Drawing

Drawing lines, both straight and wavy, is an essential prerequisite to handwriting. However, the accent should be on enjoyment rather than formal writing at 3–4 years. Thick, chubby crayons are good for producing different colour

a b c

Try tracing over the letters.

effects and patterns and are easy for your child to hold.

Many children learn to copy a variety of letters at this age. They can trace over your letters (drawn very big) or over dotted letters. Don't use capitals yet though, stick to lower-case letters.

Painting

This can take many forms and allows for lots of experimentation. Invest in some basic painting equipment, lay down some protective plastic sheets and get creative!

Ready-mixed paints are best, and are cheaply available in large plastic squeezy bottles. Pour these into small dishes or containers to allow your child easy access.

Prints Halved potatoes are useful to print patterns on paper, as are any vegetable halves, or stones, leaves and twigs.

Butterfly pictures provide a link with symmetry in maths. Fold a sheet of card or paper in half, unfold it and then let your child paint a design on one side. While the paint is still wet, fold the paper again to create a perfect reflection.

Wax designs Get your child to draw a design on paper with a stub of candle, then paint over it.

The paint clings only to the waxless portions leaving her design clearly visible.

Blow-painting put a small spot of paint in the centre of the paper then your child can blow across it with a straw to create spidery streams. Try blowing at different intensities and for different lengths to see how the patterns alter.

Scrapbooks and collages

This is the time to begin the production of 'My Scrapbook'. Your child can help you cut out items from old catalogues, magazines, comics and newspapers, and decorate her scrapbook with sticky shapes (bought in packets). The book can include photographs of your child from birth to the present day, and even include comical photographs of friends and family members. There can be pages of family visits and outings, birthdays and celebrations.

Personal experience is an ideal way to link new knowledge and experience, so explaining the items in the scrapbook periodically can be enriching. Write your child's name on the cover to give her the sense that it belongs to her.

Try including collages made of different materials. Stick in bits of patterned and coloured cloth, silver paper, leaves, sticks, coloured stones and sand. Initially you will take the lead on design, but in time your child will indicate a preference. Using stencils to draw a shape and then create, say, a collage elephant is highly appealing to this age group.

Other creative materials

These can include play-dough and plastic modelling clay. Modelling clay can be difficult and you may need to demonstrate how to cut, shape and roll it to make patterns and shapes.

Activities

1 Ask your child to count these:

a ☺ ☺ ☺ ☺ ☺ ☺

b ☺ ☺ ☺

c ☺ ☺ ☺ ☺ ☺

d ☺ ☺ ☺ ☺

2 Ask your child to copy these:

C   O   X

Ask your child to try to draw any letters or numbers you write down for her.

3 Ask your child to build a tower of wooden bricks, and to make a bridge. A tower of nine is about average for a child of three and a half.

4 Ask your child to sort knives, forks and spoons (three of each).

5 Ask your child to lay places at the table.

6 Ask your child to sort three sizes of bricks.

7 Test her on the colours: red, orange, yellow, green, blue, purple, black, white.

8 Get her to draw a girl or boy.

9 Does your child recognize letters? Try consonants: for example, b, c, d. Ask, 'What does this say?'

10 See if she recognizes any words (particularly if you have been using picture books or picture cards as suggested). Write out words clearly in lower case: cat, man, bag, dog, her name and other similar basic concrete words.

Ready for school 4–5 Years

6

Reading

By 4–5 years your child can begin reading concrete words. These words should be a combination of clear short-vowel sounds ('a' for apple, 'e' for egg, 'i' for ink, 'o' for orange, 'u' for umbrella) and describe objects that your child is familiar with. Close-matching the words with objects or ideas already in his memory is both an enjoyable and successful method for teaching reading at this age. The difficulty is that there are a limited number of words that can provide this linking experience, but the suggestions here should provide a starting-point and can be built on as your child progresses. The phonic alphabet table (right) will also be a valuable learning tool at this age.

Phonic alphabet

Your child can continue to learn the phonic alphabet in conjunction with the use of the picture cards (see page 75). To make picture cards either draw or cut out and glue a picture on to each card and write the word in clear, bold letters (lower case only at this stage) underneath. Try teaching the words five at a time for a few minutes every day.

The two major difficulties with the phonic alphabet are:

Phonic alphabet

a	for	apple	b	for	banana
c	for	cup	d	for	dog
e	for	egg	f	for	fish
g	for	gate	h	for	hat
i	for	ink	j	for	jam
k	for	kite	l	for	leaf
m	for	mat	n	for	nail
o	for	orange	p	for	pig
q	for	queen	r	for	rabbit
s	for	sun	t	for	trees
u	for	umbrella	v	for	van
w	for	witch	x	for	box
y	for	yellow	z	for	zoo

1 Relating the object to your child's experience.

2 Providing a connection in your child's mind between the sound and shape of the starting letter of the word and the sound and shape of the letter of the alphabet.

Children need to be focused on that first letter of the word – emphasize it and sound it out clearly. For examply the 'a' in apple must be pronounced correctly for sucessful learning; don't be tempted to read it as 'ay'.

a for a-pple
The picture of the apple on the picture card provides the link to experience, but the

participation of the 'a' in the structure of the word also needs to be emphasized.

When dealing with learning abstract structures – written letters and words to represent sounds and meanings – the tie-in with real life in your child's experience is vital in pegging for recall. Look for a computer programme (or set up a simple game yourself) to demonstrate what happens and how the word-structure differs when the first letter is removed.

Learning phonics

It is extremely important that the teaching of the phonic alphabet, and word shape and sound, is for only a few minutes in a learn-play session. Over a few months, this is a lot of learning, and at no stage should interest and enjoyment be sacrificed for pressing on regardless of your child's desire to participate.

Try to make this learning time as fun as possible by using entertaining pictures and creating scenarios you know your child will find amusing.

Key words (Group 1)

I, he, she, it, a, the, this, that, and, in, to, of, is, was

Key abstract words

By using word and picture cards your child will learn a range of nouns, but even in early reading the majority of words used are difficult to link to memory. They are abstract and do not all have short vowels. It is very difficult indeed to link these to a child's experience, and usually teachers of reading fall back on repeated practice (simply reading from books) to achieve recall. Try going over the Group 1 key words again and then adopting some of the methods below for sucessfully achieving recall.

The first key words were introduced on page 62, but they are also listed above (Key words Group 1) as a reminder.

Achieving recall of early abstract words

As well as practice in reading, 'pegging' is the most effective way of recalling abstract words. These can all help:

- Laying out solid letters to form the words, and then saying them out loud.

- Trace the words in a sand tray and say them out loud at the same time.

- Ask your child to close her eyes and visualize the word, saying it at the same time.

Tim is a cat

He is in the tree

Key words (Group 2)

When your child is really familiar with the key abstract words in Group 1, move on to the following words, teaching them in the same way, a few at a time.

you, him, his, we, they, all, had, have, be, are, said, as, for, at, on, with, but, not, one, so

- Make up a story in which 'a' and 'the' are the central characters, relating the details of the story to your child's experience (school, home, family, friends).
- Include the words in picture and word cards.
- You can even make short stories using the words for your child to read. Write the letters large on card with a picture.

Words need to be introduced gradually, as and when your child can recall them easily.

The range of ability (and an individual child's application) is considerable. I have known several quick-learning three-year-olds who read well, and a child of four and a half who has just begun to read. All are thrilled by the whole thing.

Choosing books

Choose reading books that have few words and large, colourful pictures, and read them with your child. The story needs to be interesting (to your child), and there should be considerable repetition of words – I can remember being totally enthralled at five years of age (and captivated by reading for life) by the story of Chicken Licken (who thought the sky had fallen on her head). The story fired my imagination, and that is the element you need to look for in books: structure that results in ease of recall. It

is a delicate balance that must be achieved, between sparking interest in the story and making learning easy by the use of sensible building blocks.

Writing letters and numbers

Small children often find letter- and number-writing laborious, so this area of learning often needs to be littered with incentives. A few become absorbed in copying, particularly if they find it easy or if practice is carefully staged and limited to only a few minutes each day. You can encourage your child's enthusiasm for writing by letting her see you write things yourself: shopping lists, envelopes, reminders, and so on. Then give her some spare paper and a pencil and let her scribble her own 'list' when you make yours. Some of her squiggles are bound to be recognizable attempts at letters, and you should praise her for these and say the letters out loud with her.

Number skills

You need to take extra care with number skills at this age, because without a link to real life, extended counting can be a failure area and the beginning of the 'I can't do maths' syndrome.

Extending counting

To practise counting, use anything appealing and ready to hand: buttons, coins (as counters rather than having different unitary values), play bricks, fingers (very useful, because they are always with you), marbles or counters. Fingers plus toes will let him count up to 20.

Fast learners are able to visualize number patterns better than slow learners, and will be able to visualize a number line such as the one shown below. This can be used as another way

of teaching counting. A number line can be written either horizontally or vertically, though the latter is preferable, since it links into negative numbers and thermometer reading later on (plus is up, minus is down).

According to your child's progress, number lines (and therefore counting) can be extended to 15, 20 or even 30 – some children are taught to count up to 100 before four years of age.

Written numbers

These can be introduced according to your child's level of attainment. Again, this varies enormously. John, at three and a half years, had effortlessly learned all number work up to 11 years (all tables, up to hundreds, tens and units; multiplying, dividing, addition, subtraction and so on). Others struggle to write numbers before they are five (especially the numbers 2 and 5, which they sometimes confuse).

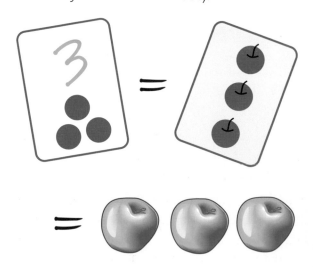

From the very beginning of number work written numbers must be related to real life, to achieve matching as close as possible. Make number cards with spots or symbols just below the number that can be counted, such as those above. Also ask your child to count whenever possible (how many cars on the road? or how many people are in the queue?) to give him a visual sense of the value of each number.

Adding

Using wooden bricks to build towers of varying heights using varying amounts of bricks provides a good link to adding. Say '1 add 1 makes 2', '1 add 2 makes 3' while moving the relevant number of bricks on top of one another.

As with all activities with young children, spend only a few minutes each day on this, but repeat it daily for as long as is necessary (unless your child's progress demands more).

Keep the numbers below 5 until the concept is firmly established. Because large numbers are more difficult to visualize, all number concepts should be taught using small numbers. Concept symbols (+, −, x, ÷) are put in last.

Number games

When your child is learning written numbers, he can play the numbers game with number cards (shown above). The aim is to make number-learning fun and to try and avoid a dislike of maths which can often develop at school age.

Throw a die and ask your child to find a card matching the number shown on the top. You can vary the game by holding up fingers and asking your child to find a corresponding number card, or ask him to put the correct number of buttons or counters on each card. You can also play the number-plate game: get your child to look at car number plates as he walks along the street with you and to identify the numbers 1 to 10 – particularly the number of his age (ask him to see how many examples of this number he can find). Get him to add up the numbers on some car number plates – is he able to find a number plate that adds up to 8? What about 10? You could also play the same game with house numbers, asking your child to add the odd and even numbers that often appear on houses on opposite sides of the street.

Adding cards

If your child is ready, you can extend the counting game to adding. Push two cards together (e.g. 1 and 2) and ask your child, 'How many now?' (see below). If she needs help show her how to find the correct card.

Number rhymes and adding stories

There are many books of number rhymes available, but you can always make up your own (always draw pictures to illustrate a simple number problem). Try the following:

'If I have two cats and go to the pet shop and get two more, how many have I got now?'

Some number rhymes have the elements of a story and can encourage counting and adding:

One man went to mow,
Went to mow a meadow,
One man and his dog,
Went to mow a meadow.
Two men went to mow,
Went to mow a meadow,
Two men, one man and his dog,
Went to mow a meadow (and so on).

A shopping game

Play a shopping game with your child. Attach labels to some of her toys with units of money written on (up to five or six units). Use large coins of the same denomination, so she can

count out the coins to you to buy the toy. Don't introduce the concept of two-unit, five-unit or ten-unit coins yet – working out change involves subtraction and demands also the rudiments of problem-solving analysis, and needs to be left until a later stage.

Shapes

Extend your child's knowledge of shapes according to her progress. If she is able, she can memorize the names of the following shapes and learn their structure by using real-life examples (window, pyramid etc.):

square, triangle, rectangle, circle, cube, cuboid, prism, pyramid cylinder, sphere.

Measurement

Teaching measurement and subsequently telling the time through play is a valuable learning method for children of 4–5 years. Soon your child will want to measure everything, from the length of a room to the weight of her toys.

Length

Play a game of 'How far across this room' with your child, and show her how to measure using strides or foot-lengths. Table tops can be measured using hand-spans. For the garden, using strips of cardboard, cut to make a metre length. Show her how to measure 'about' – 'it's about 10 sticks/6 measures/3 hands long'. Get her to compare the lengths of things – 'the garden is longer than the front room', 'my arm is longer than your arm'.

Weight

Show her how to 'weigh' things using marbles, or wooden cube blocks. You can say, 'This teddy is 12 marbles heavy', or 'This car is only 6 cubes heavy.' Get her to line objects up in order of weight.

Capacity and volume

Your child can learn about capacity by using a small plastic cup. In the bath or at the sink you can ask her to see how many cupfuls of water will fill other larger vessels. Get her to line the other object up in order of 'size' (or volume).

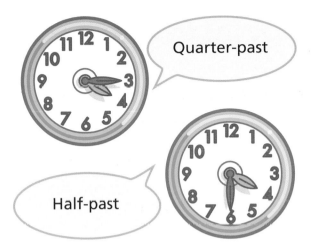

Telling the time

As soon as your child knows numbers up to 12, she can learn the time. Learning the time is surprisingly badly taught in some schools. I have found several 15-year-olds (not, by any means, all slow learners) who knew only the o'clock times. At the other end of the scale, two-year-old Luke was able to tell the time to the minute ('It's two forty-eight').

To ensure clear separation of concepts and good near-matching, telling the time has to be taught in these clearly defined stages:

1 The o'clocks until the pattern and idea are firmly established in his memory
2 The half-pasts
3 The quarter-pasts
4 The quarter-tos

A clock that has clear numbers and movable hands is essential. A good peg for linking to the passage of time is your child's ability to say when she has breakfast, dinner, tea and similar daily landmarks.

Creative play

Preschoolers are naturally creative and love experimenting – it's only with experience that they learn to plan and develop a set way of doing things. You can help your child develop his innate talents through a range of creative activities.

Drawing, colouring and painting

Your child should be very adept at using a pencil now and can draw around things. He will probably enjoy creating shapes with stencils and colouring them in. Or you can link art to maths by joining numbers to make a picture. Making symmetrical butterfly pictures also links to maths (see page 70). Folding one half of the paper over to duplicate the wet paint design on the other half of the paper results in an exact replica of what he painted.

As with the earlier age group, your child can continue making patterns on squared paper, and colour in the result with coloured pencils or fine wax crayons. Some shapes (squares, rectangles, equilateral triangles), he may discover, fit together perfectly.

Cutting out

Show your child how to use scissors to cut out pictures of toys, plants, animals and people from old magazines or catalogues. These pictures can be pasted into 'My Scrapbook'. This can also include examples of his work, or even photos or postcards that he particularly likes.

Is each half the same?

Collections

The scrapbook idea links to investigations about his local area and other areas (geographical and historical). This can be a combination of cutouts from guides and postcards of places, and even glued-in objects, such as shells, stones, pressed flowers and leaves or small mineral pieces. Such a 'topic' book can also be used to extend his vocabulary as you discuss and talk about things, and as he learns to write names.

Collage

With some help, your child can assemble a variety of objects to paste or glue to card – petals, grass, leaves, small stones, shell pieces, pieces of material, wood, coloured and shiny metallic paper, matchbox pieces, uncooked rice and macaroni, sticks and the like. He can draw a picture and build it up with collage pieces stuck into the shape, or a design made on the card with them.

Modelling

By this age your child will be able to make small models such as flowers or cakes using play-dough or plastic modelling clay – with your help. Clay-modelling sets can help interest him in creating a variety of shapes (humans, cars, animals, imaginary) as well as everyday objects.

By making shapes such as cubes, prisms and pyramids, you can show him how these three-dimensional shapes are divided symmetrically. With a plastic knife, let him cut them in half to see how each half is the same – but don't labour over it.

Constructing

Construction kits range from coloured pipe cleaners to clip-together plastic bricks and complex building sets, but even matchboxes and small cardboard boxes can be put to good use with a little help from you.

Role play and imaginative play

Dressing up and acting out stories he has heard or seen on TV and videos continues to be some of the most popular play pastimes. His dressing-up box can therefore be extended to include items that relate to whatever TV series and films are all the rage. Children this age still enjoy real-life role play, though, and so uniforms or similar (postman, policeman, nurse, doctor, secret agent) are popular.

Small toys include those of the latest craze (again, usually from TV or film), and of the staples – the farmyard, the zoo, the fire station, the shop, the home, the school. Even without small men and vehicles, children use marbles and even stones to represent people and objects.

Play-time ideas

- Read a story to your child and ask him to repeat the story to you and to explain some well-known concrete, action and abstract words.

- Ask your child to copy his name and address out (you write it down for him to copy).

- Ask your child to count these:

•	••	•••	••••	•••••
1	2	3	4	5

•••	••••	••••	••••	•••••
•••	•••	••••	••••	•••••
6	7	8	9	10

- See if your child can add these:

$$1 + 1 =$$

$$1 + 2 =$$

$$2 + 2 =$$

- Ask your child to tell you the names of these letters:

n s m l

- Ask your child to tell you the o'clock times on a clock.

- Ask your child to spot varous colours around the home.

Toys and activities

Toys, puzzles and games

Draughts
First calculator
Abacus (10 rows of 10 beads)
Weighing scales
Collage kits
Toy cash register
Magnets
Jigsaws
A B C wall charts
Word and picture cards
Clock with movable hands
Magnetic or cling numbers
Word-matching games (words with pictures)
Ruler with measurements clearly marked
Construction sets
Printing sets

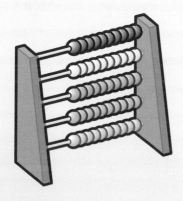

Songs

Yankee Doodle

Here We Go, Loopy Lou

The Hokey Cokey

Skip to My Lou

Michael Finnigan

This Old Man, He Played One

Little Brown Jug

Oh, Soldier, Soldier

Sing a Rainbow

She'll be Coming Round the Mountain

Amusing rhymes your child will love

I'm telling of you
Because you kissed a kangaroo
And you have never said sorry
At half-past two.

Miss Polly had a dolly
Who was sick, sick, sick,
So she phoned for the doctor
To be quick, quick, quick.

The doctor came with his hat and his bag
And he knocked on the door with
    a rat-a-tat-tat.
He looked at the dolly
And he shook his head.
He said, 'Miss Polly, put her straight to bed.'
He wrote on the paper for the pill, pill, pill,
'I'll be back in the morning with the bill,
    bill, bill.'

Ladybird, ladybird, fly away home,
Your house is on fire, and your children
  all gone.
All but the youngest whose name is Anne
And she hid under the frying pan.

Poems

'The Owl and the Pussy-Cat' *Edward Lear*

'Matilda' *Hilaire Belloc*

'Adventures of Isabel' *Ogden Nash*

'What is Pink?' *Christina Rossetti*

Films

Classic favourites include:

Alice in Wonderland
Bambi
Dumbo
Chitty Chitty Bang Bang
Fantasia
Mary Poppins
Bedknobs and Broomsticks
Jungle Book
Lady and the Tramp
101 Dalmatians
Cinderella
Pinocchio
Sleeping Beauty
Snow White
Wizard of Oz

These and similar films provide a rich memory store to draw on for storywriting. Talk about the characters and simple plot structures with your child after viewing and ask her what she thought of various aspects. The songs in films like these are especially memorable and tapes or CDs are often available to accompany the film.

Books

There are two types of books suitable for 4–5 years: those that you read to your child and those that involve her in her early reading. This is just a small selection of the many available.

You read to your child

Allan Ahlberg's *Happy Families* series and
  Red Rose Readers;

Janet and Allan Ahlberg's *Each Peach Pear Plum*

Dick Bruna books

Roger Hargreaves' *Mr Men* books

John Burningham's picture books

Beatrix Potter's *Peter Rabbit* and others

Eric Hill's *Spot* series – these have large letters
  for discovering letters and words

Jill Murphy's *Elephant Family* series

Anthony Browne's *Gorilla*

Your child reads

Any early reader series, or picture books with simple words, will engage your child. At this stage books should only have one sentence per page and plenty of brightly coloured illustrations to hold her interest and provide a link. Word and picture cards and simple A B C books continue to be useful, especially as a reference tool if your child struggles with a particular word or sound.

Starting
school 5–7 Years

7

English	88
Maths	92
Science	98
Activities	100

English

As we have seen in previous chapters there are three distinct steps in early pre-reading; reading to your child, the beginning of phonic work and the use of key words. The purpose of an organized learning system such as this is to develop good recall and stimulate interest. This system should be developed as your child progresses to achieve maximum sucess. The next steps for teaching reading are covered below.

Reading

The basis of the scheme for teaching reading to 5–7-year-olds is as follows:

- Read to your child whenever possible: ABC books, nursery rhymes, finger rhymes, jingles, fairy stories and other simple stories. Choose a book with interesting pictures and only a few lines of reading per page, and an overall interesting theme. Children will also enjoy books about real life: the zoo, the seaside, at home, at playschool, the farm, at the shops and so on.

- Books and cards with a picture and word per page or card for your child to read to you. These must relate closely to your child's experience to allow her to link to real life.

- The phonic alphabet with its link (near match) to real life: 'a for a-pple', 'b for b-anana' and so on.

- Simple words built on the phonic alphabet e.g. man, cat, dog. Grouping words by sounds, such as cat, cup and cot, is very effective.

- Cards and/or books of stories with pictures and single short sentences beneath, built on these simple words and certain key words which are extremely common in text:

  I, he, she, it, a, the, this, that, and, in, to, of, is, was

- Children will quickly learn sentences like 'the cat and the dog', written below a pasted cut-out or drawn picture. Look out for books with this approach.

Making progress

Build on this reading system with more well-constructed reading or picture books, or devise your own with a few large-lettered words per page and good coloured pictures.

Occasional words which are not of phonic derivation, or key words, can be 'read in' by you, and your child, in effect, will then have an interesting story to read. The story itself must be interesting to the age group. It should:

- be full of action
- have interesting characters
- be highly imaginative
- be funny

Further key words (which frequently occur in books) to build sentences on are

you, him, his, we, they, all, had, have, be, are, said, as, for, at, on, with, but, not, one, so

Cup **AND** saucer

Words such as these are difficult to link with a five-year-old's experience. They can be learned either by frequent repetition (reading a wide variety of stories achieves this, but progress is relatively slow), or by pegging (finding some element to match with in memory). This can be done by creating visual (mental) images in your child's mind:

cup *and* saucer

knife *and* fork

one man *and* his dog

'The dog sat on the car' creates a humorous image, and both phrases and sentences can be used to emphasize meaning.

A word like 'they' can be combined into a rhyme to help your child remember the meaning – 'They play on Sunday.'

Ask your child to close her eyes and visualize the word and also say it. She can also trace the shape of the word and try to say it.

You can extend knowledge of word shape, sound and meaning with some simple exercises. Try asking:

- Which word goes with this picture?
- Which letter must be added to complete the word that names this picture?

- Start placing key words in short sentences to give meaning:

The dog is big; the cat is not big?

Blends and vowel combinations

Once your child has mastered and become familiar with all the simple phonic sounds of consonants, you can expand into 'blends' – two consonants that come together and make one sound or syllable. Start with word beginnings such as:

cl, cr, br, bl, dr, fl, gr, gl, pr, pl, st, sp, tr, sw, sh, ch

After this, you can begin to practise some vowel combinations:

ar, oo, ee, or, er, oi, oy, ow, ou, ear

Then move on to word endings (some combinations, such as sh, ch and st, you will have encountered as beginnings):

-ng, -ll, -ss, -ick, -ock, -uck, -nk, -ect

Learning words in this way can be through exercises, or by word and picture cards.

The above activities can be linked with early writing of words, sentences and stories. The commonest nouns used in writing by early schoolers are shown over the page.

'f' and 'l' gives you 'fl' for **fl**ower

flower

house	father	garden	girl
tree	car	boat	school
flower	train	man	night
boy	doll	shop	mother
dog	baby	snow	

These are relatively easily learned for reading and by tying each word with a picture. Because of the link with real life (and, possibly, because children see the word so frequently), 'school' is spelt well quite early on.

Writing

We have seen how learning to write progresses from drawing patterns to copying and tracing one letter at a time (o and c first), to finally copying out numbers. Your child can build on this by copying a word or very short sentence that you write (to his instructions) beneath a picture he has drawn.

An excellent way of encouraging creative writing is to ask for a few words' comment on each day's happenings – a form of diary. You can discuss together what he can put (or draw).

He can also write words in his scrapbook, and try a short note to a relative or Santa Claus. Initially, his written letters and spelling will be all over the place, but leave him to develop an interest in writing, and write words for him only when he asks.

Spelling

Spelling should not be introduced until a child can read. If your child has a good background in phonics for reading then three-letter words with a central short-vowel sound will be easy to spell.

Begin this age group only with early phonic words and 'blends' that introduce words. A very effective way to teach spelling is to ask a child to cover the word after looking carefully at it and asking him to visualize it. Then get him to say the word several times, tracing the word out with his finger or writing it down, if necessary several times.

Encouraging your child to write

- Let your child see you reading and writing regularly and explain the importance. If he never sees you reading and writing he is unlikely to want to do this himself.

- Ask your child to make a list of items needed before a trip to the shops. At first you will need to help him with this but before long he'll be checking cupboards and making lists himself.

- Always talk about a book or story after reading time. If he particularly enjoys this you could ask him to write an alternative ending to the story.

- Use poetry or rhymes to demonstrate how words can rhyme and have rhythm. Encourange him to list words that rhyme. He may also be able to write simple poems at 6–7 years.

- Play word games with your child. Say aloud or write words with some of the letters mixed up and ask him to try and guess what they are.

- Use words that sound like their subject, such as splat, roar and yelp. Ask him to pronounce them while imagining the action.

- Try introducing him to longer words such as symmetrical, longevity and release. Explain their meaning and ask him to form a sentence using the words.

Words for spelling practice (short vowel words)

Spelling should not be tested until reading is well established. If pre-school has been good, then these first two groups at six or seven years of age should be easy. Teach also key words, and words most common in writing

Group 1

man	bat	sad	bag	ham	cap
can	cat	dad	lag	jam	gap
ban	sat	bad	rag	ram	lap
fan	fat	had	tag	sam	map

Group 2

men	bet	bed	beg	hem
den	met	led	leg	
pen	pet	fed		
ten	set			

Group 3

ibin	bit	bid	big	hip	him
din	fit	did	dig	pip	rim
tin	hit	hid	fig	lip	dim
fin	kit	kid	pig	sip	

Group 4

not	pod	bog	cop
cot	cod	hog	mop
hot	god	dog	lop
pot	nod	log	top

Group 5

bun	but	bug	gum	cup	bud
fun	cut	dug	hum	pup	dud
nun	gut	rug	mum	sup	mud
pun	hut	hug	rum		

Double blend beginnings

These form a second fairly easily recalled set of words (especially if words are chosen which relate to experience, and can be pictured).

grab	grip	grin
clam	clap	
cross	crab	
blob	blot	
dress	drop	
flip	flag	
frog		
glad		

Word middles

rain	train	sail
bark	shark	
boot	moon	
book	cook	
feet	sheet	
fork	horse	
coin	boil	
card	dark	

Word endings

cash	rush	bush
drill	still	hill
wing	sing	king
long	song	
drink	stink	

Magic 'e'

This changes a short vowel to a long one.

rid	ride
rod	rode
tub	tube
cap	cape

Maths

It is very important that your child doesn't associate early maths with any sense of failure. Much failure in schoolwork is rooted in the first two years of schooling. To avoid failure, concrete representations must accompany abstract symbols for as long as necessary. Use real-life objects, pictures, diagrams, number lines – anything that can be physically counted – alongside numbers, to link the concrete to the abstract.

Adding

You can teach this using cards or wooden bricks. Counting on the fingers (for answers up to 10) is also excellent. At some point, though, the use of real-life objects must tie in to use of abstract symbols.

Counting will link numbers of things to written numbers, but the '+' symbol also needs to be linked to 'pushing things together'. Also, the '='

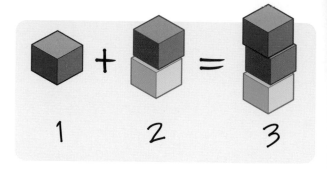

sign must be clearly matched in your child's mind with 'the same as' or 'balance'. A little practice with a short number line (0–5) will get a child used to this. For:

2 + 3 = 5

use the vertical number line. Start on 2, and then count up 1 to 3, count up 2 to 4, then count up 3 to get to 5.

Number bands

Speed in number work is increased considerably if children build into their memory instant recall of 2 + 3 = 5, 4 + 5 = 9, and so on. Such knowledge is very useful for later number work.

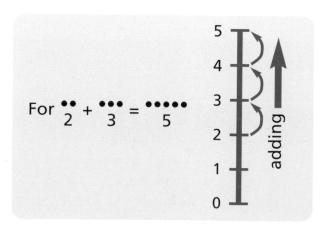

For example:

3 x 8 = 8 x 3

38 + 23 = 23 + 38 = 61
and 61 – 23 = 38 and 61 – 38 = 23.

Grasping this will also lead to searching for useful patterns in real life, such as dealing with money and change, or measuring things.

Variations

One of the most important variations in 'adding sums' is the change from working horizontally to working vertically. For some children this is a considerable modification to what they have in their memory to match against. Each format produces a different mental image, and to link these you will need to explain the new process and also point out similarities in both. Also, the old format can be continued in practice exercises while the new is being introduced.

Taking away

Rhymes can help your child to understand that subtraction is the removal of objects. Try 'acting out' the following rhyme with your child:

$$\overset{||}{2} + \overset{|||}{3} = \overset{|||||}{5}$$

$$\begin{array}{r} \overset{}{2} \;|| \\ + \; 3 \;||| \\ \hline 5 \;||||| \end{array}$$

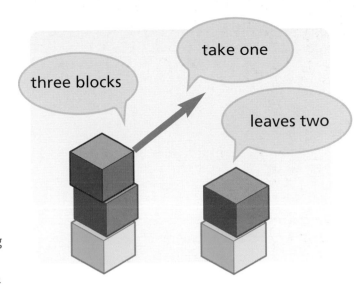

Two little dicky birds sitting on a wall,
One named Peter, one named Paul.
Fly away, Peter
Fly away, Paul.
Come back, Peter
Come back, Paul.

Use your fingers, or finger puppets, to act out the flying away and return of Peter and Paul and get your child to count the birds at each stage.

Near-matching with the abstract symbols causes difficulty. Show her with your fingers: 3 take away 2 is three fingers up, count two down, leaves one. Then, show her on paper:

'Instead of fingers we can write down 3 spots'

O O O

'And then we take away 2 spots. Let's cross them out. How many spots does that leave?'

O Ø Ø

The next stage is to substitute numbers:

'We write the number 3 for 3 spots, and then the take-away sign and then the number 2 for the 2 spots we take away. And that makes …

3 – 2 = 1

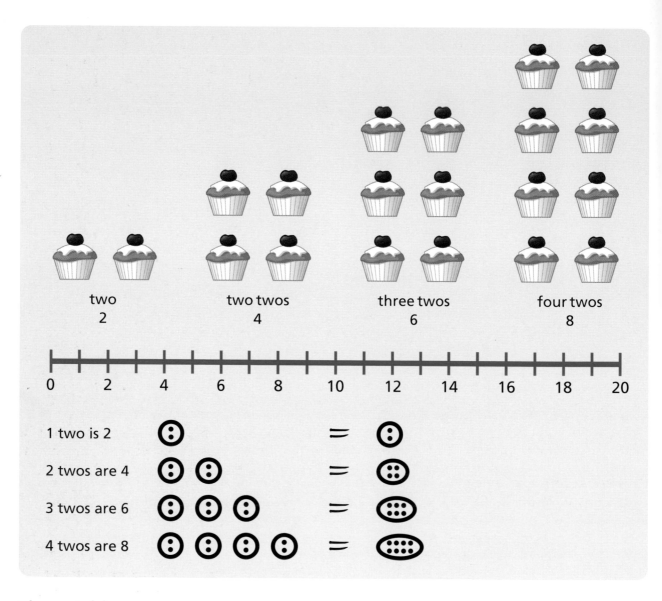

two	two twos	three twos	four twos
2	4	6	8

1 two is 2

2 twos are 4

3 twos are 6

4 twos are 8

Times tables

As with adding and subtraction, use real-life objects and diagrams to assist visualization.

According to your child's experience, these approaches should create a clear modifying mental image that may also be a 'peg' for easy recall.

The 2 times table provides a good opportunity to talk about odd and even numbers. Make a numbers table (see pages 61 and 110) to show how every number is alternately even or odd, that an even number + 1 makes an odd number, and so on. This helps signpost the way to other number patterns later.

Time

Days of the week and months of the year
Help your child learn the order and spelling

with frequent repetition and 'pegs' such as rhymes:

Solomon Grundy,
Born on Monday,
Christened on Tuesday,
Married on Wednesday,
Took ill on Thursday.
Worse on Friday,
Died on Saturday,
Buried on Sunday,
That was the end of Solomon Grundy.

Thirty days hath September,
April, June and November;
All the rest have thirty-one,
Excepting February alone,
Which has but twenty eight days clear
And twenty nine in each leap year.

The clock

This was talked about in previous chapters, but many children begin to learn it at this time. Stages in the teaching are:

1 There is a long hand (minute) and a short hand (hour). The minute hand moves faster than the hour hand – this needs to be shown on a clock, or a good model of a clock.

2 The o'clocks need to be practised first.

3 Then practise the half-pasts.

4 Next, the quarter-pasts.

5 Then the quarter-tos.

Once these landmark times are clear, teach that there are 60 minutes to the hour, 30 to the half-hour, 15 at the quarter-past and 45 at the quarter-to. This stage is multi-phased and takes some time to learn. As your child learns the 5 times table, counting round the clock becomes much easier.

The two halves of the apple make a whole.

Early fractions

Teach the idea of 'half' (and that two halves make 1) by cutting through symmetrical objects such as cakes, buns, oranges, apples, moulded play-dough shapes, and showing diagrams and pictures.

Once the idea of 'half' is clear, show him how in the same way the half of a half is a quarter and that four quarters make 1.

Money

This should be taught in the following stages:

1 Practise adding up one-unit coins first and using them in a 'shop' with you, a friend, or brothers and sisters.

2 For multiple-unit coins, tap the required amount of times on the coin.

3 Arrange shopping to involve only buying things with correct money.

4 Once he is adept at this, teach the giving of change by pricing 'shop' objects low (such as a teddy for two units) and buying one object at a time.

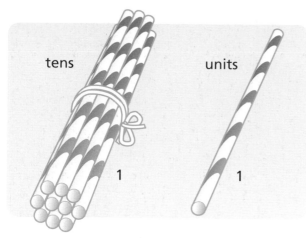

Tens and units

The learning of tens and units provides a link to counting. Try the following:

- Take 11 objects, for example, wooden bricks or straws, and place them in a pile.

- Ask your child to sort out 10 and build a tower or lay them in line.

Say, 'That is one 10 and one unit.' Then write down the abstract form:

TENS   UNITS
1   1   is 11

Buttons and similar small objects also teach the concept well. Using straws is particularly useful, because ten can be tied up with cotton or wool.

The process can be repeated for 12, 13, 14, 15....

You can then show her how amounts over 20 make two 'tens' piles and so on (see also pages 104–5), which will prepare her well for adding larger numbers.

Measurement

Building the concept of measurement and its 'modifications' into your child's memory is best done in the following stages.

Begin with the concepts of distance, weight and capacity without using units. As described in the previous chapter, distance can be measured using steps or hand-spans; weight by the number of marbles or wooden cubes on a weighing balance; and volume by the number of plastic cupfuls needed to fill containers.

Once this stage is understood, introduce the idea of units.

Length
Choose a ruler with units clearly marked off (look for one with alternate bands of coloured stripes rather than just marks along the edge). and show your child how to measure things.

Weight
Replace marbles by weights and let her use these to measure to the nearest whole unit. Your child will only need to say, 'The book weighs 8 weights.'

Capacity
Replace the plastic cups used earlier with a volume measure. Your child can then say, 'Six

measures fill a plastic jug – nearly.' Measuring capacity doesn't need to be exact at this stage. Detailed calculations will wait until she is proficient in hundreds, tens and units, but providing this half-way step means she will be familiar with the tools by the time she moves on to specific units of measurement.

Shapes

Shape recognition should be established at 5–7 years. Your child should recognize the following:

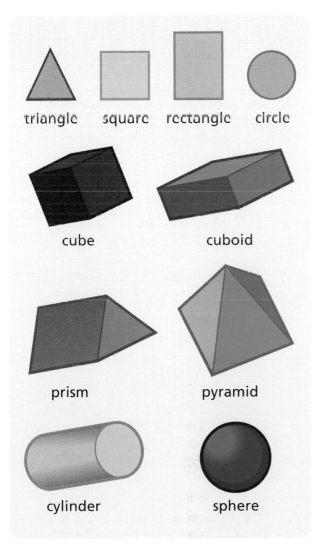

triangle   square   rectangle   circle

cube   cuboid

prism   pyramid

cylinder   sphere

Reflective symmetry

Learning to recognize symmetry and being alert to mirror images and repeated patterns is helpful to later number work. Butterfly pictures (familiar from previous chapters) illustrate the idea well. This concept can be explained further by looking for lines of symmetry in capital letters.

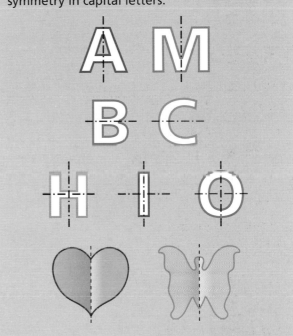

Angles

A pair of compasses (with the point removed) or even a door being opened against a wall explains the concept of 'angle'. The wider apart the 'arms', the bigger the angle.

Rotation and the points of the compass link to the idea of angles. Mark the four points of the compass on a large sheet of paper. Your child can stand in the centre and experience the 'rotation' as she turns, for example, from north to east, south to west.

Science

A little science was touched on in the previous chapters and at 5–7 years this can be developed further. Build on those same subjects, both in more detail and with the use of more sophisticated words and larger sentences, to extend his areas of knowledge.

Growth

Sow cress seeds in damp sawdust or soil in a container on a window sill. Growth is fast, so your child can observe changes each day and even (with a 6–7-year-old) write about what he sees. You can explain about roots, stems and leaves. Relate this growth to the growth of trees, flowers and grass.

How are the ladybird and the flower different?

The plant gets bigger as it grows – just like me!

Your child can also observe (or write about) pets as they grow from kittens or puppies to full-grown animals, and perhaps observe baby animals at a farm or a zoo. Some television programmes, including those aimed directly at children, bring experiences of growth of animals into the home that your child could never hope to observe in real life.

The variety of life

You can begin to use and provide encyclopedias for your child: books about birds, the zoo, the seaside and nature in general.

Your child can search the garden or park for a variety of animals (such as ants, beetles, woodlice, spiders, caterpillars, ladybirds). Answering questions that your child asks is important, as is any extra input that you can provide with these answers. Details of animal classification are not important – even at much higher levels in school life precise details are not required – but you can teach their names, how the animals live, what they eat. Gather some groups of pictures and real animals and plants to help make what you say memorable.

- Worms, insects, spiders, shellfish, fish, amphibians, reptiles, birds, mammals. Always be sure your child returns even worms and insects to their natural environment.

- Mosses, ferns, seaweeds, flowering plants, trees (include those with flowers and those with cones).

Also make your child aware of the dangers of wasps and bees, and of eating certain berries.

People are different
Point out how people differ:

eye colour, hair colour, shape, height, feet/hand size, child/adult differences, skin colour.

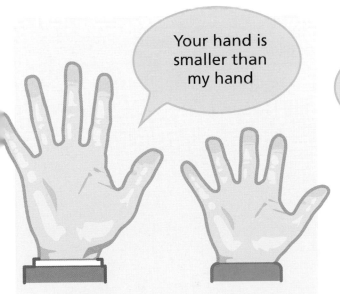

Your hand is smaller than my hand

Areas of knowledge

- Parts of the body
- Health and hygiene
- Forces
- Looking after the environment
- Sorting materials
- The seasons
- Weather

As well as real-life examples, look out for some of the excellent books about these subjects. Your child will also begin to be able to record what he discovers, which might be in the form of a graph or pictogram, or as a diary or a straight account in a scrapbook.

Solids, liquids, gases

An excellent way to demonstrate that at different temperatures substances are either solid, liquid or gas is to take an ice-cube, warm it in a saucepan until it changes to water, and boil the same water until steam is produced.

Ice is a solid, water is a liquid and steam is a gas

ice   water   steam

Activities

English

No. 1

a Ask your child to read out loud the letters of the alphabet (she can sing the alphabet, but must try to sound them out phonically).

b Ask her to copy the alphabet in upper and lower case.

c Ask her to write her name and address.

d Ask her to name the items listed below. Ask, 'What is this?'

On the body
shoulder, ankle, wrist, cheek, chin, stomach, chest, eyebrows, eyelashes

In a room
settee (or sofa), vase, saucepan, light, chair, table, television, books, shelves

Food
onion, carrot, cabbage, tomato, lemon, grapes, bread, pasta shapes, potato, tins

No. 2

a Ask your child to read these words aloud:

man   ten   bun   pot   sit
the   and   here   was   go
into   car   bus   tree

b Ask her to do these actions (or explain): hop, dig, scrub, polish.

c Ask your child to explain: warm, a nap, leaning, snow, a tree, an elephant. (The quality of answer gives some indication of her knowledge, and also of her command of language.)

d Ask your child to put the right word under the pictures:

car   tree   house

No. 3

a Ask your child to put the right word under the pictures:

moon   plate   feet   crown   hat

b Ask your child to name these parts of the face by pointing to the picture below.

hair   eye   nose   ear   mouth

c Ask your child to read these words:

he   to   of   was   that
and   the

my   go   on   are   far
had   have   him   his   hot
one   said   see   some   so
they   went   with   we   you

No. 4

a Ask your child to match the words to the pictures below:

apple table fork pram chair
spoon grass swing frog food
boots ship door television brush

b Ask your child to read these words aloud:

as   at   be   but   all

No. 5

a Get your child to read out loud to you from a picture book with simple text. Ask her to explain what is happening on each page, and (at the end) to tell you the gist of the story (in simple terms).

b Ask your child to copy these words:

house	father	garden	
girl	tree	car	boat
school	flower	train	man
night	boy	doll	shop
mother	dog	baby	snow

c Ask your child to put the right words under the right pictures (not all words have a picture):

walk run jump dig hot cold
big little up down sad happy

No. 6

a Ask your child to name these things on his own body:

mouth, lips, hand, arm, elbow, wrist, foot, leg, ankle, shoulder, knee, neck, chest, stomach, chin, cheek, eyebrow, eyelash, forehead

b Ask your child to write the number words in order. The first one is done for you:

1	2	3	4	5
one	_	_	_	_

6	7	8	9	10
_	_	_	_	_

Choose from:

two five six three eight
nine seven four ten

c Ask your child to match the right word with the right picture:

table chair apple car television (TV) swing fork door brush

d Ask your child to spell:

cat   mat   hat   pan   rat   dad
sad   jam   cap   tap   sat   at

e Ask your child to write the days of the week in order (start with Sunday):

Tuesday Friday Monday
Saturday Thursday
Wednesday Sunday

f Ask your child to spot the following colours at home: red, orange, yellow, green, blue, purple, black, white, grey.

Maths

No. 1

a Ask your child to count these:

1   2   3   4   5

b Ask your child to name these shapes and copy them:

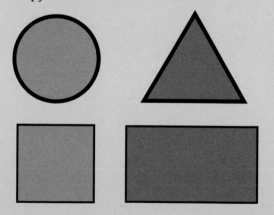

Choose from these words:

circle triangle rectangle square

No. 2

a Ask your child to count these:

f f f f f f

u u u u u u u

b b b b b b b b b

n n n n n n n n

e e e e e e e e e e

b Ask your child to copy these numbers:

1   2   3   4   5   6   7   8   9

10   11   12   13   14   15   16

17   18   19   20

No. 3

a Ask your child to count these:

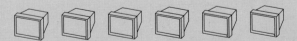

b How many altogether?

• and •• is ____

•• and ••• is ____

No. 4

a Ask your child to count these:

b Ask your child to add these:

$1 + 1 =$ __ $2 + 1 =$ __ $3 + 1 =$ __

$2 + 2 =$ __ $3 + 2 =$ __ $4 + 2 =$

$3 + 3 =$ __ $4 + 3 =$ __ $5 + 3 =$ __

$5 + 5 =$ __ $5 + 4 =$ __ $4 + 4 =$ __

$6 + 1 =$ __ $6 + 2 =$ __ $6 + 3 =$ __

No. 5

a Ask your child to do these sums:

••••• + •••••• = ____
5   6

•••••• + •••••• = ____
6   6

••••••• + ••• = ____
7   3

••••••• + ••••• = ____
7   5

•••••••• + ••••• = ____
8   6

b Tell your child to use the number line to add:

4 + 7 = ___

7 + 7 = ___

8 + 7 = ___

9 + 4 = ___

8 + 8 = ___

8 + 6 = ___

9 + 8 = ___

5 + 9 = ___

9 + 9 = ___

9 + 6 = ___

6 + 7 = ___

```
20
19
18
17
16
15
14
13
12
11
10
9
8
7
6
5
4
3
2
1
0
```

c Ask your child to name these shapes:

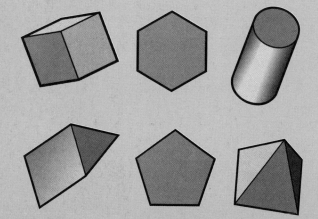

Choose from:

cube   prism   hexagon   cylinder

pentagon   pyramid

No. 6

a Ask your child to do these take-away sums:

3 – 1 = ___   4 – 3 = ___

OOØ   OOØØ

5 – 3 = ___   4 – 1 = ___

OOØØ   OOOØ

b Ask your child to do these sums:

4 + 6 = ___   5 + 3 = ___

7 + 8 = ___   9 + 9 = ___

8 + 3 = ___   9 + 7 = ___

5 – 2 = ___   4 – 3 = ___

4 – 1 = ___   3 – 2 = ___

☐ + 1 = 3   2 + ☐ = 5

c Use a 10 x 10 abacus to count up to 50, 60, 70, 80, 90, 100.

No. 7

a Ask your child to put these in order with the smallest first:

7   2   8   3   12   4   17

b What are these numbers?

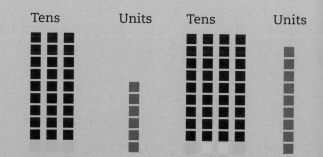

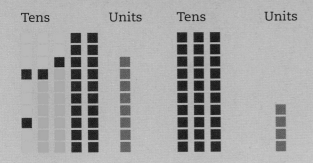

Tens	Units	Tens	Units

c Ask your child to use the abacus to continue these patterns:

2 4 6 8 _ _ _ _ _ _

10 20 30 40 _ _ _ _ _

10 15 20 25 30 _ _ _ _

c Ask your child which is her left and which is her right hand.

d Tell your child to mark the even numbers:

1 4 7 8 6 10 15

e Tell your child to mark the odd numbers:

2 6 3 9 4 12 8 5

f Ask your child to tell you the times on these clocks.

No. 8

a Get your child to repeat the pattern below, without looking:

2 4 6 8 10 12 14 16 18 20

b Ask your child to do these sums:

1 x 2 = ___   2 x 2 = ___

3 x 2 = ___   4 x 2 = ___

5 x 2 = ___   3 x 2 = ___

5 x 2 = ___   4 x 2 = ___

No. 9

a What fractions are the shaded parts?

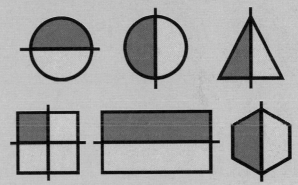

b Ask your child to count the number of chairs, tables and beds in your home.

How many more chairs are there than tables?

How many tables and beds are there altogether?

c Ask your child to draw the lines of symmetry in the capital letters of the alphabet:

A B C D E F G H I J K L M

N O P Q R S T U V W X Y Z

Note some are vertically symmetrical, some are horizontally symmetrical, some are both, and some have no symmetry.

At school

7–9 Years

8

English

By this age your child should have a good grasp of language and this will be covered extensively in school. However, you can continue to accelerate his progress at home using the following methods.

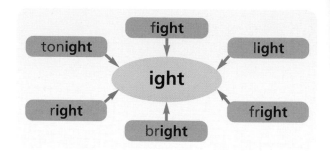

Reading

If your child is not reading fairly well by seven years old, something is wrong. Progress can be accelerated by working through the reading exercises in Chapter 7, or by teaching him yourself using phonic and other methods discussed there.

A child of average reading ability will need interesting stories with humour (especially when adults in authority make fools of themselves), adventure, magic or other excitements in them to further interest. As with all ages (including adults), good characters in books, and a good story, will develop a general interest in reading. However, stories need to be fairly short and words a little bigger than in adult books. Some children will still prefer books with interesting, colourful pictures with only a few sentences of reading per page. Others may have a stronger imagination, and create their own mental pictures from the words and sentences in the story.

Continue reading with your child, if he wishes it, and also if it assists when he is falling behind. Ensure reading time is fun, never a chore, and be sure to choose books he will enjoy and find stimulating.

Spelling

Word middles cause the greatest difficulty in spelling. Learning ten at a time, once a week works well. Slow learners may prefer it if like-structured words are set out in a 'webbing' or schematic way, shown above.

Silent letters
Get your child to visualize the word with the silent letter floating away from it:

and returning again:

Try linking sight and sound of the 'phoneme' (sounding syllable) with real-life meaning:

or   au
s___c e   s___c e

Try asking 'Do you want sorce or sauce?'.

Spelling and useful writing words

The following words should be used for practice in forming sentences. Investigating the use of words and constructing longer pieces of writing should also be encouraged.

Long vowels

able	we	ice	no	unit
radio	even	island	go	usual

Blends and silent letters

see		
coin	join	
boy	toy	
sea	eat	leaf
head	bread	dead
boat	soap	road
rain	train	sail
day	say	play
out	shout	cloud
how	down	clown
lamb	climb	thumb
hour	ghost	rhyme
bright	tonight	right

know	knee	knife		
write	wrist	wrong		
cry	fly	try	shy	
sing	ring	fling	king	
happy	mummy	silly	daddy	
when	why	who	where	what
fight	sight	light	night	fright

Useful writing words

birthday yesterday picture because
aeroplane television brought tomorrow
morning afternoon wood bonfire
rocket colour football castle elephant
sometimes dinosaur whale shark
pretty firework church through queen
catch cry cried hospital breakfast fair
doctor bicycle please animal knock
magic ready wheel grass caught
build monkey pair write something
clean head garage teacher engine
won snowman bread kitten harvest
piece cousin chair balloon change
together picnic front mouse

Writing

Structured writing should be clearly defined by 5–7 years but further teaching is still required. The development of good writing skills comprises the five elements listed below:

1 Adequate handwriting
2 Word knowledge and spelling
3 Sentence construction, grammar and punctuation
4 Paragraphing
5 Good ideas ordered appropriately

Some of these elements can be learned through exercise, practice and 'pegging' for recall, but the ideas themselves need to be applied in practice. There needs to be a 'balance' between knowledge of structure and freedom to express creative ideas.

Encourage your child to write creatively (some children may need help with getting started, while others may be full of ideas) but ensure the five elements are adhered to. Paragraph structure and the ordering of ideas can be particularly problematic.

Maths

By 7–9 years your child should have a firm grasp of addition and subtraction and should be progressing well at telling the time with confidence. Number work will be covered in school but teaching at home can now begin to take a more structured approach.

Large numbers and place value

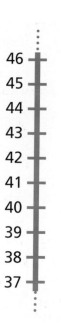

Counting needs to be continued so that your child has a visual record in memory of numbers like 45, and the number line from 37 to 46: with this in memory 38 + 6 and 43 – 4 are easy to work out.

Look at the position of numbers like 25, 50, 75 as being ¼, ½, ¾ along from 0 to 100. Exercises can reinforce the meaning of the 5 and 2 in 52, for example.

Arrays

Arrays can be used in conjunction with a 10 x 10 abacus to show that 74 + 10 = 84, 56 + 20 = 76 or 93 – 20 = 73.

Addition array

1	2	3	4	5	6	7	8	9	10
11	12	13	14	15	16	17	18	19	20
21	22	23	24	25	26	27	28	29	30
31	32	33	34	35	36	37	38	39	40
41	42	43	44	45	46	47	48	49	50
51	52	53	54	55	56	57	58	59	60
61	62	63	64	65	66	67	68	69	70
71	72	73	74	75	76	77	78	79	80
81	82	83	84	85	86	87	88	89	90
91	92	93	94	95	96	97	98	99	100

Times tables can also be picked out for recall, particularly the 5 times tables and 10 times tables. Use of an array gives not only a facility wih number bands, but also a sense of the deeper meaning of large numbers.

Multiplication arrays

These arrays are particularly valuable as a basis for unit conversion later – 10 times and 100 times as shown here for decimal measures, but you can make others for other bases: 8 times, 12 times, 14 times and so on.

Multiplication array

	1	2	3	4	5	6	7	8	9	10
x 10	10	20	30	40	50	60	70	80	90	100
x 100	100	200	300	400	500	600	700	800	900	1000

The clock and time

The final stages in the learning of time are intervals of less than 15 minutes, different ways of expressing time and calculating the passage of time.

Counting in 5s around the clock
Practice with the clock can include times like 7.10 and 7.50.

Expressing time
An additional complication to telling the time is the fact that we have different ways of referring to 'minutes to' and 'minutes past' the hour. For example, 7.50 is 10 minutes to 8. This means further practice using a different modifying image.

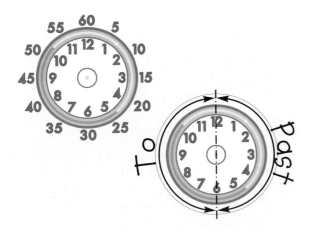

The passing of time
A problem such as 'How long is it from 10.30 to 10.45?' can easily be explained by showing your child how to count on the clock. You can then teach your child to work out a question like: 'How long is it from 10.30 a.m. to 2.15 p.m.?'

Setting out sums

Check that your child understands the conventions for laying out adding and subtracting in sums:

	Tens	Units			Tens	Units
	2	4			7	6
+	3	3		–	2	4
	5	7			5	2

Carrying and borrowing

Using straws to 'bundle up' tens together with abstract symbols and sum structures works best. The concept of carrying is shown below:

	Tens	Units
		7
+		4
	1	1
	1	

is

a bundle of ten

Maths 111

Borrowing is the reverse of this process:

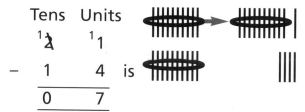

Tens   Units

$^{1}\cancel{2}$ $^{1}1$

−   1   4   is

―――――――――

0   7

Multiplication

A sum like 24 x 2 is best translated into:

Tens   Units
  2   4
x   2

―――――――――

―――――――――

and then broken down as

Tens   Units
  2   4
x 2   x 2

―――   ―――

  4   8

―――   ―――

to show the answer:

Tens   Units
  4   8

This step needs to be mastered before moving
to something that requires addition to the tens,
like: 25 x 2

Tens   Units
  2   5
x 2   x 2

―――   ―――

  4   10

―――   ―――

This gives an extra ten, so 4 tens and the extra
ten is 5 tens = 50

The right-hand unit sum can later be written as:

Units
  5
x 2

―――

  0

―――

Eventually, the two parts are brought together:

Tens   Units
  2   5
x 2   x 2

―――   ―――

  5   0

―――   ―――

Division

Division can expressed in two ways.

$2\overline{)12}$ and $12 \div 2$

Your child should link to both the question:

'How many twos in 12?'

or

'How many if I share 12 between 2 people?'

Remainders
Step 1 What happens when 5 sweets are shared
between 2 people?

2 each and 1 left over

Step 2 Show how this can be represented by

$$2 \overline{)3\,{}^{1}2}{}^{\displaystyle 1\,6}$$

Tell your child that, instead of putting remainder 1, the remainder goes on to the next number (strictly speaking, of course, this is transferring a ten).

Fractions

The relation between fractions is important to establish: that there are two eighths in a quarter, two quarters in a half and so on. Also your child needs to know that:

a half of 8 is 4

a quarter of 8 is 2

three-quarters of 8 is 6

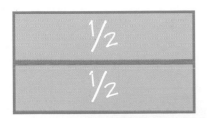

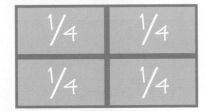

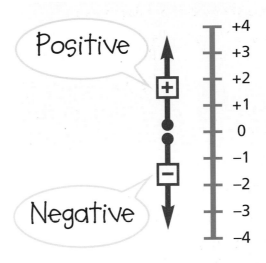

Negative numbers

The idea that counting backwards does not stop at zero can be totally fascinating to children. Show your child that the thermometer goes down below 0°.

The calculator

Your child can use a calculator to check his answers, and also to investigate addition and subtraction of large numbers:

1000 + 1000 + 1000 = 3000

20,000 – 5000 = 15,000

Multiplication and division have an even more dramatic effect on numbers:

20,000 ÷ 1000 = 20

5 x 1000 = 5000

Most important is to include some insight into place value:

5 x 10 = 50, 5 x 100 = 500, 5 x 1000 = 5000 etc.

(also 5 x 10 is 5 with a nought added = 50).

Science

Teaching science to children of this age will be an extension of the pre-school teachings and at 5–7 years. Concepts and facts already developed in the child's mind are expanded upon as her knowledge grows.

Animal groups

Use a wide variety of books (check out sales, school fairs and the library as well as bookshops) to explore with your child a variety of animal groups and their characteristics.

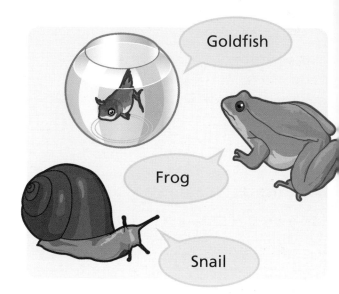

Goldfish

Frog

Snail

Animal groups

Insects
insects have six legs

fly ant beetle bee wasp
moth butterfly

Snail group
all have a soft body

slug snail
cockle winkle
mussel whelk

Crab group
both have a hard shell

crab lobster

Worms
worms have segmented bodies

earthworm
lugworm ragworm

Fish
fish live in water and have gills

shark cod goldfish herring
carp mackerel

Amphibians
amphibians have slimy skin and can live on water and land

frog toad newt

Reptiles
reptiles have scaly skin

crocodile alligator
snake lizard

Birds
birds have feathers and can fly

eagle sparrow
blackbird

Mammals
mammals are warm-blooded

ape monkey cat dog
cow pig elephant
whale dolphin

Forces in everyday life

These include lifting, pushing, pulling, kicking, butting, throwing. Your child can look for forces in sports – tennis, soccer, athletics, swimming, skiing, boxing, wrestling, judo.

There are also forces in cars, planes, trains, ships, rockets, the wind, earthquakes, volcanoes, tidal waves, waterfalls, landslides.

There are stored forces in springs, elastic bands, yo-yos and so on.

Vibrations

There are several ways of producing vibrations:

- Hold the end of a ruler on a table and 'pluck' the end hanging over the edge. Vibrations travel through the table as well as the air.
- Blowing across the top of an empty bottle or one partially filled with water produces vibrations in the air in the bottle.
- Straws cut at one end produce vibrations, shorter straws having higher notes.
- Rolling a single marble into a line of marbles (all touching each other) illustrates how vibrations pass through materials, producing a 'knock-on' effect.
- All musical instruments create vibrations and thus sound. Your child can look at and experiment with a variety of instruments to see how they produce vibrations: piano, violin, guitar, drum, xylophone, recorder, trumpet, clarinet, harp, cymbals …

An electrical circuit

Join a small battery to a bulb and get your child to investigate whether various materials conduct electricity: wood, metal, pencil, lead, cloth, rubber, plastic, paper. Use the materials to complete the circuit through the bulb from one terminal on the battery to the other.

Living things

All living things respire, feed, move, multiply, excrete waste products, react to the environment and grow. Your child will appreciate these as they apply to her – she gets bigger, she moves, eats and drinks, breathes, excretes, has reactions (hot things hurt, for example), and when she grows up may have children.

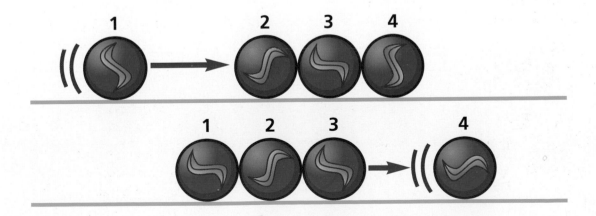

Activities

English

No. 1

Opposites Ask your child to match the correct words to the pictures:

fat/thin   big/little   hot/cold
up/down   sad/happy   right/wrong
heavy/light   day/night

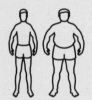

No. 2

a What am I?

I bark

I purr

I moo

I tick

I quack

I drip

Your child can choose from:

cat tap duck cow dog clock

b Who am I?

I drive a bus

I catch fish

I look after people in hospital

I fly a plane

I look after people's teeth

I teach children

Your child can choose from:

**dentist bus-driver pilot
fisherman nurse teacher**

No. 3

a Name these groups:

Car, bus, train, bike

Ant, bee, fly, ladybird

Coat, hat, shirt, trousers

Apple, orange, banana

Rose, daisy, daffodil

Shark, goldfish, cod

Your child can choose from:

fish fruit clothes insects flowers transport

b Mark the odd one out:

Eye, finger, foot, hat, hair

Shoes, dress, socks, curtains

Milk, potato, water, lemonade

Car, bus, whale, toy, train

c Arrange in order of size, smallest first:

8, 3, 9, 11, 1, 72

Eight, two, nine, six, a half

Bus, car, pram, ship

Year, hour, second, minute, day

No. 4

a Cat is to kitten as dog is to

Hand is to arm as foot is to

North is to south as east is to

Cup is to saucer as knife is to

Cake is to eat as milk is to

Shoe is to foot as glove is to

Your child can choose from:

fork drink leg hand puppy west

b Unjumble the underlined words:

At school we do **smus** in maths.

I like **edabr** and butter.

We like to swim in the **eas**.

I go by **usb** to school.

The leaves fell off the **eter**.

I like to eat bread and **seeche**.

No. 5

a Ask your child to put capital letters and full stops in the following:

on sunday my family and i went to the seaside my friend philip came too we went to the fair and my dad had a ride on the big dipper when he got off he had a green face and said his stomach was in his head later philip bought a comic and while he was reading it he walked into the boating lake it was certainly lucky the water only came up to his knees or he would have drowned

b Ask your child to unjumble these sentences:

school to am going I?

much how those are sweets?

teacher my witch is nasty a.

day I one bed wrong the out got side of.

No. 6

a Ask your child to correct the wrongly spelt words:

skool plaice wear you goes to lurn.

my teecher she tries to teech us fings, like maths and topics.

b Ask your child what word the following refer to:

A hundred years

The day before tomorrow

What you were doing before you woke up

My father's father is my...

No. 7

Comprehension Ask your child to read the passage and answer the questions below:

That night, Sammy made himself a sandwich for supper.

'I can't unscrew this jar top,' he said. 'I wish I were stronger.'

'When I was your age,' said Grandpa, 'I was so strong that I used to bend a lamp-post to read my comic better, and wrestle fifteen gorillas with an arm tied behind my back and still win easily. That's how strong I was.'z

'I don't think so,' said Sammy.

From *When I was Your Age* by Ken Adams (Simon & Schuster, 1991)

Questions (write answers in sentences)

Why can't Sammy unscrew the jar top?

What time of day is it?

How many gorillas did Grandpa wrestle?

How did Grandpa read his comic?

Is Grandpa telling the truth?

Does Sammy believe him?

No. 8

a **Writing a letter** Ask your child to write a formal letter starting 'Dear …' and finish with 'Yours sincerely'.

b **Storytelling** Ask your child to finish off this story:

The day I turned into a giant

One day, I woke up and my feet were sticking right out of the bed and across the room.

'Why is my bed so small?' I asked myself. Even the room looked tiny. I climbed out of bed, and then bumped my head on the ceiling …

c **Word puzzle** Ask your child to find these words in the word puzzle:

car bike bus train ship plane
ant laugh an and chin be

The words all appear in a straight line, but you can go diagonally and use some of the same letters twice.

g	r	e	e	p	k	b
r	s	b	u	s	a	t
s	h	i	p	z	n	r
c	g	k	s	a	z	a
h	u	e	a	n	d	i
i	a	c	a	r	i	n
n	l	p	l	a	n	e

Maths

No. 1

a Ask your child to do the following addition sums:

```
  4  ••••        7  •••••••
+ 2  ••        + 5  •••••
____           ____

____           ____
```

```
     T U               T U
  •• 2 3  •••      •••• 4 2  ••
+  • 1 2  ••      +  • 1 3  •••
  _____           _____

  _____           _____
```

b Ask your child to tell you what the number 6 in 649 stands for.

c Ask your child to multiply the following:

7 x 2 = ___   5 x 2 = ___

4 x 2 = ___   9 x 2 = ___

3 x 10 = ___   4 x 10 = ___

8 x 10 = ___   7 x 10 = ___

2 x 5 = ___   4 x 5 = ___

9 x 5 = ___   7 x 5 = ___

d Ask your child to do the following subtraction sums:

```
  7  •••••••        8  ••••••••
- 2  ••           - 3  •••
____              ____

____              ____
```

```
 10  ••••••••••
-  5  •••••
____

____
```

```
 T U        T U        T U
 7 6        8 9        9 7
- 2 4      - 3 4      - 4 5
_____      _____      _____

_____      _____      _____
```

e Ask your child to tell you the times on these clocks:

No. 2

a Ask your child to multiply the following:

```
  4        7       10        5
x 2      x 2      x 2      x 2
___      ___      ___      ___

___      ___      ___      ___
```

b Ask your child to do the following additions:

```
 T U        T U        T U        T U
 2 1        1 3        3 2        1 3
+ 2 9      + 2 7      + 4 8      + 3 8
_____      _____      _____      _____

_____      _____      _____      _____
```

c Ask your child to do the following subtractions:

```
 T U        T U        T U        T U
 7 2        8 0        7 3        4 3
- 1 6      - 1 2      - 2 5      - 1 6
_____      _____      _____      _____

_____      _____      _____      _____
```

d Ask your child to give answers to the following:

$5 + 5 + 2 = $ ___

$10 + 5 + 5 = $ ___

$10 + 10 + 2 = $ ___

$50 \times 10 + 2 = $ ___

e Ask your child to do the following subtractions:

$20 - 16 = $ ___ $50 - 27 = $ ___

f Ask your child to do the following multiplications:

$$\begin{array}{cccc} 15 & 16 & 25 & 36 \\ \times\,2 & \times\,2 & \times\,2 & \times\,2 \\ \hline \\ \hline \end{array}$$

No. 3

a Ask your child to write 110 cm in metres.

b Ask your child to tell you how many centimetres there are in 1.24 metres.

c Ask your child to add together 1.20 and 0.80.

hint
$$\begin{array}{r} 1.20 \\ +\ 0.80 \\ \hline \end{array}$$

d Ask your child to tell you what 5 x 50 cm is in metres.

hint
$$\begin{array}{r} 0.50 \\ \times\ \ \ \ 5 \\ \hline \end{array}$$

e Ask your child how many 2s there are in 8?

No. 4

a Ask your child what ½ of 6 is.

b Ask your child what ½ of 8 is.

c Ask your child to do the following divisions:

$\frac{1}{2}$ of 16 = $2\overline{)16}$ = ___

$\frac{1}{2}$ of 14 = $2\overline{)14}$ = ___

d Ask your child to tell you the times on these clocks:

e Ask your child what number needs to be added to 6 to make 14.

f Ask your child to do the following sums:

$$\begin{array}{r} 3\ 2\ 4 \\ +\ 1\ 3\ 5 \\ \hline \end{array} \qquad \begin{array}{r} 8\ 4\ 9 \\ -\ 1\ 3\ 4 \\ \hline \end{array}$$

$$\begin{array}{r} 2\ 2\ 3 \\ \times\ \ \ \ \ \ 2 \\ \hline \end{array} \qquad \begin{array}{r} 2\ 1\ 3 \\ \times\ \ \ \ \ \ 4 \\ \hline \end{array}$$

No. 5

Ask your child to do the following division sums, expressing the answers as X remainder Y where the answers are not whole numbers.

$2\overline{)3}$ $2\overline{)5}$ $3\overline{)4}$

$3\overline{)5}$ $2\overline{)30}$ $2\overline{)32}$

No. 6

a 1 hour = ___ minutes

b ½ hour = ___ minutes

c ¼ hour = ___ minutes

d Ask your child to name this angle:

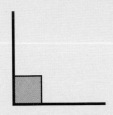

e Ask your child to estimate the height of a door.

f How many right angles are there in turning:

  a From N to E?

  b From N to S?

  c From E to N?

g Ask your child to tell you the answers to the following:

  a What is 3 more than –1?

  b What is 5 less than 2?

  c 3 – 7 = ___

h Ask your child to do the following sums:

$$
\begin{array}{ccc}
48 & 17 & 14 \\
\times\,2 & \times\,3 & \times\,5 \\
\hline
6 & 1 & 0 \\
\hline
\end{array}
$$

$5\overline{)80}$ $4\overline{)60}$

i Ask your child what number comes next:

  a 1, 3, 5, 7, ___

  b 7, 5, 3, ___

j Ask your child to complete the other halves of these symmetrical letters (same on each side of the dotted line):

k Ask your child to tell you how many halves there are in:

  a 2 whole ones?   = ___

  b 2½? = ___

l Ask your child to tell you how many quarters there are in:

  a 2 whole ones?   = ___

  b 2½? = ___

Growing in confidence

9

9–11 Years

English

As well as continuing to develop spelling, punctuation and grammar, children of 9–11 years should be encouraged to write descriptively. Writing stories with structured plot-lines and character development should be encouraged and can be an enjoyable pastime. Other children may prefer to write about real experiences in the form of a diary or news book.

Descriptive writing

I can't think what to write,' says Philip. I suggest things to write about, story titles and even start a story for him, but he is still lost over how to structure what he wants to write. You can make suggestions like this, and start your child off by writing the first few sentences (as in the exercises at the end of this chapter).

Children should also know, though, that a story should capture the readers' interest from the beginning. The beginning needs to introduce characters and situations and link to the main part of the story – the middle. Characters should be in conflict with something – others, the environment, the supernatural, even with their own thoughts and feelings. There needs to be humour (if possible) in the narrative, action and it should appeal to the senses.

Encourage them to write both about things they know and also about pure fantasy.

Punctuation

It is important that your child uses the correct punctuation when writing and doesn't get into bad habits. Speech marks and commas can be confusing and you should encourage your child to follow the rules below.

Speech marks
Question marks and exclamation marks are included within speech marks:

- 'Why?' asked the man.

- 'Stop that!' he shouted.

- 'My name is Jack,' he said.

Commas
- These are used for lists: 'There were cows, pigs, horses and dogs.'

- For breaks within a sentence: 'Fred, the new driver, met us at the shop.'

- Sometimes used before 'but', 'or', 'nor', 'for': 'He asked if he could have a cake, but I gave him bread.' or 'I love doughnuts, for they're so

Spelling – homophones

These are words sounding alike but with different meanings.

aloud	allowed	find	fined	mare	mayor	right	write
ball	bawl	flour	flower	meat	meet	ring	wring
beach	beech	groan	grown	medal	meddle	road	rowed
bean	been	hair	hare	missed	mist	sail	sale
beat	beet	heal	heel	none	nun	scene	seen
blew	blue	hear	here	pail	pale	son	sun
brake	break	heard	herd	pair	pear	sore	saw
buy	by	him	hymn	pause	paws	stair	stare
cell	sell	hole	whole	peace	piece	steal	steel
cereal	serial	hour	our	peal	peel	tail	tale
scent	sent	knew	new	peer	pier	their	there
coarse	course	knight	night	plain	plane	threw	through
currant	current	knot	not	rain	reign	tide	tied
dear	deer	knows	nose	raise	rays	vain	vein
fair	fare	lead (metal)	led	rap	wrap	waist	waste
feat	feet	made	maid	read	reed	weak	week

delicious.' Here, 'for' is used as a reason, but when used in its dative sense 'for' has no comma preceding: 'I invite you for tea.'

Spelling

Homophones (word which sound alike but have different meanings) such as those listed above can be introduced to spelling practice at this stage. It may take lots of practice and several attempts for your child to instinctively use the correct spelling but with careful work and a patient approach this should come naturally.

Once the different meanings and spellings of the above have been grasped your child can begin making up sentences using these words and eventually progress on to including them in stories and descriptive writing.

Be sure to check that your child is using the correct form of the word and the correct spelling in the right context.

Further creative writing

Once your child has a grasp of descriptive writing you can help her to develop this skill and encourage further creative writing.

Start by suggesting your child imagines a scene in her mind and then prompt her by asking what she sees:

> The fair was a blaze of colour – red, blue and gold roundabouts, and striped stalls, and lots of brightly coloured flags at the entrance.

And are there sounds in the scene?

> In the black of the hallway, Dan heard a sound that stopped the beating of his heart. It was the long, terrifying creak of the slowly opening front door …

Other senses to be involved could be taste, touch and smell, although only as part of the action and storyline.

Speech can help identify a character:

> 'Er, what are you, er, hiding from?' asked the little girl, who always sounded nervous.

The use of action verbs ('He ran up the stairs …') is better than the use of neutral ones ('He went up the stairs …').

Wherever possible a reference to the passing of time adds interest

> He remembered when, as a small boy, he had peered through those curtains, and watched the rag-and-bone man trundle his cart down the narrow street …'

although your child at this age may have a sense of history going back only a few years.

Finally, a story needs to build up the conflict to a climax. Remind your child of how this happens in fairy stories, such as when the woodcutter kills the wolf in 'Little Red Riding Hood', or how her favourite stories and films have an exciting part near the end, and there should be a short resolution (of the sort, maybe, 'They all lived happily ever after.').

There are other forms of descriptive writing that should be encouraged too. These include diaries, poems, accounts (of trips, holidays and so on), and, simply, a stream of consciousness. There is also the essay form: 'Why I like go-kart racing' or 'How I would change school'. Writing something she enjoys or wants to say will encourage fluency.

The suggested words and phrases on page 127 may be useful in encouraging your child to develop her writing skills, particularly if she finds story-writing an onerous task.

Ideas for creative writing

While story-writing can be an enjoyable pastime for some children, others may find it difficult to grasp. In this case the following two pointers may help.

- **Poems and rhymes** Ask your child to try using some of the homophones listed on page 125 to make up amusing poems and rhymes. She could write these out neatly and add drawings to illustrate the 'story'.

- **Everyday activities** The journey to school, a trip to the shops or attending an after-school activity will probably seem unremarkable to your child, but ask her to imagine the unthinkable occuring (her favourite music or sports star coming to school, for example) and you've got the beginnings of a story.

Useful words and ideas for descriptive writing

Describing people

Figure tall short fat thin frail athletic

Face round oval long thin fat wrinkled

Nose long fat snub straight broad

Hair straight wavy curly coarse fine bald

Eyes large small beady shifty sparkling

Skin pale swarthy fair bronzed ruddy freckled

Mouth, lips wide thin rosebud

Teeth stained bad decayed irregular projecting uneven

Character kind proud vain greedy selfish miserable affectionate honest humble charming spiteful mean loyal generous sincere lovable stubborn obstinate timid bold impetuous

Habits and characteristics quizzical worried troubled laughing giggling sneering twitching

Voice high-pitched squeaky shrill hoarse deep harsh grating rasping husky nasal

Actions walking running leaping clapping writing drawing painting hitting hanging sawing chopping

Sounds

People shouting crying weeping laughing screaming chattering shrieking tutting giggling groaning moaning muttering whistling singing

Nature leaves rustling thunder clapping rain beating wind rushing steam hissing water dripping

Animals mice squeaking bees buzzing dogs barking cats mewing cows lowing sheep bleating horses neighing lions roaring birds singing

Around the home television blaring tap dripping fire crackling food frying water boiling clock ticking door creaking

Smells
Flowers burnt toast hot cakes perfume old socks gas

Taste
Sweet sour bitter tasty nasty

Touch
Caress stroke fondle kiss hug squeeze rub pound prod poke

Colours
Green grass red roses yellow daffodils blue sky blue sea yellow sand silver moon golden sun white clouds

Country scenes
Trees fields rivers hills farmyard church

Town scenes
Roads streets offices shops road crossings traffic railway station

Coast
Sand shore waves pier fair roundabouts big wheel rocks cliffs caves fish yachts rowing boats liners hotel pebbles sea breeze deck chairs

Rooms
Shape decoration windows ceiling carpet rug fire lamps lights furniture

Maths

Maths will be an important part of your child's school work at 9–11 years and vital for success at examination time. Gentle encouragement and non-oppressive teaching methods will work wonders for the reluctant mathematician.

More tables

By this age your child should have a firm grasp of the times tables. The 7 and 8 times tables are often the hardest to learn and your child may need some extra help with these. Grouping, as described earlier, may help and can also provide a link to division.

In the 9 times table there are clear patterns which can help your child to work out the answers.

On each line the addition of the digits equals 9 (e.g. $0 + 9 = 9$, $1 + 8 = 9$, $2 + 7 = 9$) and the units go down by 1 as the tens go up by 1.

$$3 \times 9 = 27$$

▼ units (9 to 0)

```
 1 x 9 = 0 9
 2 x 9 = 1 8
 3 x 9 = 2 7
 4 x 9 = 3 6
 5 x 9 = 4 5
 6 x 9 = 5 4
 7 x 9 = 6 3
 8 x 9 = 7 2
 9 x 9 = 8 1
10 x 9 = 9 0
```

▲ tens (9 to 0)

Counting on the fingers of both hands also reveals the 9 times table. For example, for $3 \times 9 = 27$, hold both hands face down in front of you. Count 1, 2, 3 from the left on the left hand, and tuck that finger in. The fingers to the left of the tucked-in finger are the number of tens and the number of fingers to the right are the number of units.

Further work on fractions

Equivalence

Understanding fraction equivalence can be tough. The table on page 129 and sums below may help your child to understand.

1							
½				½			
¼		¼		¼		¼	
⅛	⅛	⅛	⅛	⅛	⅛	⅛	⅛

$\frac{1}{2} + \frac{1}{2} = 1$

$\frac{1}{4} + \frac{1}{4} + \frac{1}{4} + \frac{1}{4} = 1$

eight $\frac{1}{8}$ make 1 whole one

Also $\frac{1}{2} = \frac{2}{4} = \frac{4}{8}$ and $\frac{3}{4} = \frac{6}{8}$

Later this can be linked to:

$$\frac{1 \times 2}{2 \times 2} = \frac{2 \times 2}{4 \times 2} = \frac{4}{8} \quad \text{and} \quad \frac{1 \times 4}{2 \times 4} = \frac{4}{8}$$

The link with decimals

This area is one of the least well understood in the whole of maths. Links to real life are needed, or children will find it difficult to visualize large numbers, so it is a subject that must be staged thoughtfully, with careful consolidation at each stage.

This square may help your child to visualize the relationship of decimals to whole numbers and to fractions.

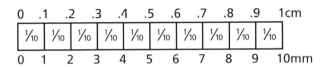

Also:

$.7 = \frac{7}{10}$ $.07 = \frac{7}{100}$ $.007 = \frac{7}{1000}$

Exercises of the type, 'How much of 1 cm is 4 mm, as a fraction, and a decimal,' are very effective.

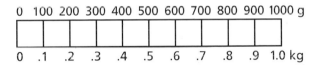

1 cm = 10 mm and 1 mm = 0.1 cm are relatively easy to illustrate for visualization (and thus near matching). 1 metre = 100 cm is more difficult, but can be linked to measurement using a 1 metre rule, and also to the grid in stage 2.

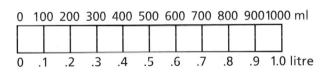

0.01	$\frac{1}{100}$	$\frac{1}{100}$	$\frac{1}{100}$	$\frac{1}{100}$	$\frac{1}{100}$	$\frac{1}{100}$	$\frac{1}{100}$	$\frac{1}{100}$	$\frac{1}{100}$	$\frac{1}{100}$	0.10
0.11	$\frac{1}{100}$	$\frac{1}{100}$	$\frac{1}{100}$	$\frac{1}{100}$	$\frac{1}{100}$	$\frac{1}{100}$	$\frac{1}{100}$	$\frac{1}{100}$	$\frac{1}{100}$	$\frac{1}{100}$	0.20
0.21	$\frac{1}{100}$	$\frac{1}{100}$	$\frac{1}{100}$	$\frac{1}{100}$	$\frac{1}{100}$	$\frac{1}{100}$	$\frac{1}{100}$	$\frac{1}{100}$	$\frac{1}{100}$	$\frac{1}{100}$	0.30
0.31	$\frac{1}{100}$	$\frac{1}{100}$	$\frac{1}{100}$	$\frac{1}{100}$	$\frac{1}{100}$	$\frac{1}{100}$	$\frac{1}{100}$	$\frac{1}{100}$	$\frac{1}{100}$	$\frac{1}{100}$	0.40
0.41	$\frac{1}{100}$	$\frac{1}{100}$	$\frac{1}{100}$	$\frac{1}{100}$	$\frac{1}{100}$	$\frac{1}{100}$	$\frac{1}{100}$	$\frac{1}{100}$	$\frac{1}{100}$	$\frac{1}{100}$	0.50
0.51	$\frac{1}{100}$	$\frac{1}{100}$	$\frac{1}{100}$	$\frac{1}{100}$	$\frac{1}{100}$	$\frac{1}{100}$	$\frac{1}{100}$	$\frac{1}{100}$	$\frac{1}{100}$	$\frac{1}{100}$	0.60
0.61	$\frac{1}{100}$	$\frac{1}{100}$	$\frac{1}{100}$	$\frac{1}{100}$	$\frac{1}{100}$	$\frac{1}{100}$	$\frac{1}{100}$	$\frac{1}{100}$	$\frac{1}{100}$	$\frac{1}{100}$	0.70
0.71	$\frac{1}{100}$	$\frac{1}{100}$	$\frac{1}{100}$	$\frac{1}{100}$	$\frac{1}{100}$	$\frac{1}{100}$	$\frac{1}{100}$	$\frac{1}{100}$	$\frac{1}{100}$	$\frac{1}{100}$	0.80
0.81	$\frac{1}{100}$	$\frac{1}{100}$	$\frac{1}{100}$	$\frac{1}{100}$	$\frac{1}{100}$	$\frac{1}{100}$	$\frac{1}{100}$	$\frac{1}{100}$	$\frac{1}{100}$	$\frac{1}{100}$	0.90
0.91	$\frac{1}{100}$	$\frac{1}{100}$	$\frac{1}{100}$	$\frac{1}{100}$	$\frac{1}{100}$	$\frac{1}{100}$	$\frac{1}{100}$	$\frac{1}{100}$	$\frac{1}{100}$	$\frac{1}{100}$	1.00

1 kg = 1000 g and 1 litre = 1000 ml can be shown diagrammatically using a number line of 100 units.

Each square represents $\frac{1}{100}$ of the big square

$0.01 = \frac{1}{100}$ and $0.10 = \frac{10}{100} = \frac{1}{10}$

$0.02 = \frac{2}{100}$ and $0.20 = \frac{20}{100} = \frac{2}{10}$ etc.

Place value can also provide an additional modifying link:

Problem work in fractions

Children of this age answer readily to 'What is half of 8?'. It is easily visualized and has been well pegged and near-matched by this stage. 'What is half of 52?' can cause difficulties, and the link between fractions and division needs to be made:

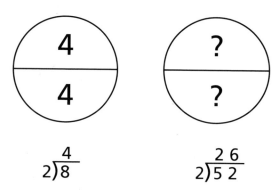

$$2\overline{)8}^{\;4}$$

$$2\overline{)5\,2}^{\;2\,6}$$

'What is ¼ of 52?' causes more difficulty:

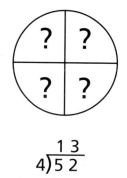

$$4\overline{)5\,2}^{\;1\,3}$$

¾ of numbers also needs to be linked carefully:

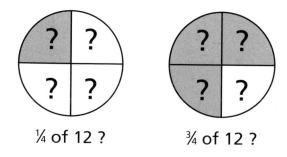

¼ of 12 ?   ¾ of 12 ?

Again, each stage needs careful consolidation.

Working totally in the abstract is the use of a process:

¾ of 12   top   3
              bottom 4

12 divide the bottom (4) $4\overline{)1\,2}^{\;3}$

times the top (3)   3 x 3

Angles

These can be investigated both on the compass and on the clock:

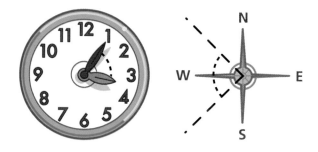

A pair of compasses can illustrate the size of named angles:

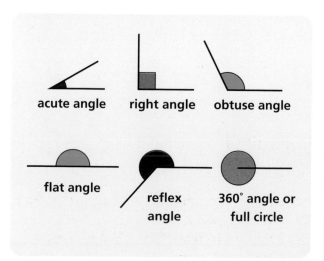

acute angle   right angle   obtuse angle

flat angle

reflex angle

360° angle or full circle

Perpendicular, horizontal and vertical

Examples:

perpendicular	horizontal	vertical
	floor	door
	table top	wall
	chair seat	chair legs
	sea surface	tree trunk
		tower

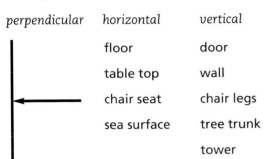

the arrow is perpendicular to the line

Rotation

Draw the points of the compass on a large sheet of paper. Pin a smaller square piece of paper centrally on top of it, as shown. As the corner a is turned through b and c to position d, your child can see where the man ends up (c, d, a correspond to 90°, 180°, 270° rotations).

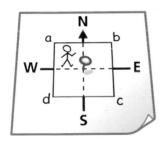

Probability

No chance	Half-chance	Certainty
I will not be born	Tossing a coin	I am reading this
I can jump to the moon	I am male or female	I have a parent

Average (mean)

The link with sharing is a useful one.

If 8 sweets are shared between 2 girls in the way shown on the left (above) it seems 'unfair'.

Fairer is shown on the right.

The average of 5 and 3 is 4. The average is called the mean. The general concept of average is illustrated using several sweets and several people.

More than, less than

This is usually expressed as:

8 is bigger than 3 $8 \geq 3$

3 is smaller than 8 $3 \leq 8$

The bigger number always occupies the wide part of the sign and the sign always points to the smaller number.

Science

Science teaching in school will typically fall into the areas of biology, chemistry and physics as your child progresses to post-11 education. The activities and areas of investigation below will form a firm basis for this while remaining enjoyable.

Biology

The following biological studies will be both useful and enjoyable for a child of this age.

The parts of a plant
Investigate with your child the parts of a plant and their functions (e.g. stem, leaf, flower, petal).

The organs of the body
With the help of a model or illustration discuss the positions and functions of the various organs of the body (e.g. heart, kidney, liver).

Reproduction
Reproduction can be difficult to grasp. Use the following simple facts to help him understand.

Animals The young of mammals are called babies, kittens etc. depending on the species.

Plants Flowers produce pollen, which is carried by wind and insects to other flowers, and a seed is produced.

Fruits Fruits contain seeds (e.g. tomato, apple, pear, orange, lemon, raspberry, melon) which grow into new fruits.

The plant has leaves, flowers and petals.

Nuts Nuts themselves are large seeds (e.g. walnut, Brazil nut, coconut, peanut) which naturally fall to the earth or can be planted.

Cones Cones contain seeds: if planted these grow into a new plant.

Health and environment
Children of this age should begin to understand that external factors can have an adverse affect on our health and environment.

Pollution comes from car fumes, factory smoke and other poisons. Discuss the effects of pollution with your child and how the various chemicals can damage our environment.

Germs Some 'germs', called viruses, cause diseases (colds, chickenpox, measles). Injections (vaccination) can prevent some of these illnesses.

Physics

Your child needs to know about the different types of materials and their properties as well as physical states, the weather, the solar system and forces.

Materials and physical states

Get your child to think of additions to the following lists:

Everyday materials

stone brick cement pottery metal glass
paper rubber leather cloth hair wool
plastic graphite

Physical states

Solids	Liquids	Gases
ice	water	steam
iron	milk	air
wood	petrol	
stone	oil	
sugar		

Uses of metals

Iron/steel	bridges cutlery pipes
Aluminium	saucepans aircraft
Copper	wires pipes
Zinc/tin	prevent iron from rusting
Copper	ornaments buckles buttons

Uses of plastics

Plastic/ rubber/PVC	shoes clothes tablecloths toys
Polystyrene	packing insulation
Perspex	in place of glass

The weather

You and your child can investigate the following topics together:

Weather recording instruments

Include rain gauge, barometer, anemometer (measures wind speed), weather vane (shows wind direction).

Weather hazards

Include hurricanes, tornadoes, whirlwinds, frost, drought, monsoon, rain, hail.

Other topics

The Beaufort Scale
The greenhouse effect
The water cycle
Clouds
Fronts
Acid rain

The solar system

Investigate together:

Our sun and its planets
Meteors and asteroids
Eclipses (of sun and moon)
Comets

Forces

You and your child can investigate together materials of different densities but similar size (such as piece of iron, modelling clay, marbles). Introduce the idea of gravity pulling down on things using the following topics:

Weight and balance
Pulleys
See-saws and levers

Activities

English

No. 1

a Comprehension

Wilbert eventually reached the would-be Wizard, who seemed paralysed, and peered over his shoulder. What he saw was the most terrifying sight that he could ever have imagined.

Facing the old bag-of-bones Wizard, standing in a mound of leftover bones from previous meals, was the largest reptile this world has ever seen. It was alligator in shape, but far bigger, and the head was the size of a T. Rex. It opened its mouth and showed row upon row of gleaming razor-sharp white teeth, each tooth the size of a knight's broadsword. It roared, and the sound echoed around the room like a deep roll of thunder.

'Gargantua,' muttered the transfixed Merlog. 'The Beast of Beasts.'

From *Wilbert and the Wiz* by Ken Adams

Questions (your child should write the answers in sentences)

Who was Wilbert trying to get to?

What does 'paralysed' mean?

What was the Wizard standing in?

What type of animal's head was the monster's head like?

How big were the monster's teeth?

What was the monster's roar like?

What was the monster called?

How do you think Wilbert was feeling?

b Ask your child to make sentences with the opposites of these words:

answer	cheap	bright	difficult
early	empty	honest	success
entrance	many		

No. 2

a Ask your child to correct the spelling, punctuation and grammar in this letter:

I'm sorry that I coodn't put your letter up the chimnee this is becos we got no chimnee only central heating so I sent the letter to yore home in lapland

for christmas I wants a motor-bike like my big bruther got then I can foller spies and things like that

my dad keeps saying all he wants for christmas is a win on the lottery so he wont hav to work no more and my mum ses that she don't want him around the house all day becos his socks stinks up the place to much perhaps its best you don't giv him no christmas present
luv
Samson Superslug

From *Samson Superslug*, Ken Adams (Orca Books, 1996)

b Ask your child to choose the correct word to fill in the spaces in the following sentences:

The wind _____ the tree down.
blew, blue

The blue _____ was bobbing in the bay.
boy, buoy

We paid our _____ on the bus.
fair, fare

It was the winter _____ from school.
brake, break

The sunflower is a very large _____.
flower, flour

Look over _____ and you will see him.
their, there

No. 3

a Ask your child to put these into the
   past tense:

   The girls are going to the fair.
   The bells are ringing.
   I am going to town.
   The boy falls down.
   You go to town.
   Are you writing the letter?

b Ask your child to make everything in these
   sentences plural:

   The boy runs in the race.
   The man plays tennis.
   I am going on my holiday.
   The lady is cleaning her house.
   The footballer kicks the ball around
      the defender.
   My friend buys me a present.

c Ask your child to write down words similar in
   meaning to these and to make sentences out
   of them:

commence conversation difficult abandon
conceal imitate maximum

No. 4

a Ask your child to write down the opposites of
   these words and make sentences with them:

   loud hate somewhere peace few rough
   hard permanent false hide

b Ask your child to put these sentences in the
   right order to make a story:

   We went to the fair.
   Everybody got in the car.
   After the fair we had ice-creams.
   We got ready to go.
   My brother and I went on the Big Dipper.
   We went home.
   Dad said we could go to the seaside.
   We reached the seaside.

c Ask your child to finish off the sentences in
   at least five words:

   The car was moving fast . . . .

   I woke up suddenly . . . .

   The boy fell in the water . . . .

   The man crept . . . .

   The teacher was cross because . . . .

d **Comprehension**

There was a second, louder rumble. The
ground beneath our feet began to tremble
and heave.
  'Back to the steps!' said Sue, with sudden
desperation in her voice, and we all turned
and ran stumbling down the narrow passage.
  'Help me,' pleaded Sol from behind. I

turned, and saw him struggling beneath the weight of the old box. Sue saw him, too.

'The place is falling in on us and you try to save some old box,' she shouted – but we could see that Sol wasn't going to give it up. Sue grasped one end and I held it underneath.

There was an almighty crash from behind.

'The room's collapsed,' said Sol.

With difficulty, we reached the steps and began to climb.

Then I remembered.

'Roger's not here,' I said. 'We left Roger behind.'

Sue looked at me, sudden sadness in her eyes.

'It's no good,' she said. We can't go back.'

I stared back at the choking cloud of dust as we struggled up the stone steps. Then, from out of the crumbling stonework dashed a blur of brown mongrel.

'Roger!' I gasped. 'You dodger!'

From *The Ghost Killer Gang* by Ken Adams

Questions (your child should write the answers in sentences)

Why were the children getting desperate?

Why was Sol falling behind the other two?

How did Sue and the narrator help Sol?

Why was there an 'almighty crash'?

Who had been left behind?

What sort of an animal was Roger?

Why did the writer call Roger a 'dodger'?

What sort of place do you think the children were in?

No. 5

a Ask your child to correct these sentences:

I work more harder.
The man what went there was a spy.
He is the oldest of both of us.
I cannot go no further.
I have forgot the time.
She were at home.

b Ask your child to put at least five words at the beginning to make sentences:

. . . . I bumped my head.

. . . . and then they caught him.

. . . . swim.

. . . . by mistake.

. . . . very happy.

c Ask your child to put in punctuation marks:

Yesterday I had some sweets there were chocolates mints and caramel

You go home she said or your Mum will be cross

For Christmas said the boy I am going to have a computer game a train set some money and a football

Maths

No. 1

a Ask your child to do the following sums:

$$
\begin{array}{r} 7\ 1\ 2 \\ +\ 8\ 9\ 8 \\ \hline \\ \hline \end{array}
\qquad
\begin{array}{r} 8\ 4\ 2 \\ -\ 3\ 7\ 6 \\ \hline \\ \hline \end{array}
\qquad
\begin{array}{r} 9\ 0\ 1 \\ -\ 1\ 7\ 3 \\ \hline \\ \hline \end{array}
$$

$$\begin{array}{r} 1\ 2\ 6 \\ \times\ \ \ \ \ 3 \\ \hline \\ \hline \end{array} \qquad \begin{array}{r} 4\ 8\ 6 \\ \times\ \ \ \ \ 4 \\ \hline \\ \hline \end{array} \qquad \begin{array}{r} 7\ 4\ 9 \\ \times\ \ \ \ \ 6 \\ \hline \\ \hline \end{array}$$

b Ask your child to put in numbers: seven hundred and twenty-three.

c Ask your child to write in words: 617.

d Ask your child to do the following divisions:

$3\overline{)27}$ $\qquad$ $3\overline{)54}$ $\qquad$ $4\overline{)96}$ $\qquad$ $2\overline{)532}$

e 240 = ? x 24 _____

f A boy has three lessons – maths, English and science. He can have them in any order. Ask your child to write down all the different combinations he can have.

No. 2

a What is the chance of getting a head when you toss a coin?

b How many hours is three lots of 40 minutes?

c Ask your child to change to decimals:

$\frac{1}{10} =$ ____ $\qquad$ $\frac{3}{10} =$ ____ $\qquad$ $\frac{7}{10} =$ ____

$\frac{4}{10} =$ ____ $\qquad$ $\frac{1}{100} =$ ____ $\qquad$ $\frac{3}{100} =$ ____

$\frac{7}{100} =$ ____ $\qquad$ $\frac{17}{100} =$ ____ $\qquad$ $\frac{34}{100} =$ ____

$\frac{85}{100} =$ ____ $\qquad$ $\frac{21}{100} =$ ____

d Ask your child to change to fractions:

0.1 = ____ $\qquad$ 0.7 = ____

0.01 = ____ $\qquad$ 0.08 = ____

0.15 = ____ $\qquad$ 2.03 = 2 ____

e $\frac{1}{10}$ of 1 metre = $10\overline{)100}$

f $\frac{3}{10}$ of 1 metre = $10\overline{)100}$ x 3 = ____

g $\frac{7}{10}$ of 1 metre = $10\overline{)100}$ x 7 = ____

(Tell your child: divide by the bottom, times by the top)

No. 3

a Ask your child to do the following divisions:

$7\overline{)63}$ $\qquad$ $8\overline{)72}$ $\qquad$ $9\overline{)54}$

b What is ¾ of 20?
(Tell your child: divide by the bottom, times by the top)

c A father is three times as old as his son. How old is the son if the father is 36?
(Hint, if needed, that: ? x 3 = 36 is the same as 36 ÷ 3.)

d Ask your child to change to 24-hour times:

7.30 p.m

2.00 p.m.

8.30 p.m.

e ¼ of £2.00 = _____
¾ of £2.00 = _____

No. 4

a Ask your child to do the following divisions:

$3\overline{)1161}$ $\qquad$ $7\overline{)1015}$

b Timetable

Station	Train 1	Train 2	Train 3
Blimpton	11.35	12.55	14.24
Sandown	11.53	13.14	14.39

Which train is the quickest?

How long does it take?

A man gets to the Blimpton station at 1.15.
How long will he have to wait for a train?

c Ask your child to draw the nets of:

A cube.

A prism.

d Ask your child to mark these points and join up the points to make a shape:

(2, 1), (2, 3), (3, 4), (4, 3), (4, 1), (3, 0)

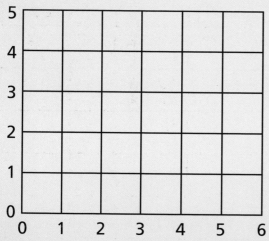

(**Hint** the horizontal coordinate along the bottom of a graph or map reference is always given first, then the vertical coordinate.)

e What is ¼ of 1000 ($= 4\overline{)1000}$)_____

f What is ¾ of 1000 ($= 4\overline{)1000}$ x 3)_____

g What is the chance of getting a '6' if I throw a die?

No. 5

a How many right angles are there if you turn clockwise from east to north?

b Ask your child to name these angles (obtuse, acute or reflex):

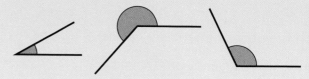

c Ask your child to tell you how many degrees there are between the hands on the clock.

d 23 x 10 =   23 x 100 =

40 ÷ 10 =   400 ÷ 10 =

e How many hundreds in 400?

How many hundreds in 40,000?

f Ask your child to name three objects perpendicular to the floor.

g If you face south and turn through 180° (two right angles), where are you now facing?

h Ask your child to add 7.1 + 2.9 _____

No. 6

a What is the mean of these numbers?

   2 5 7 8 3

   (**Hint** Add them together, then divide the total by the number of numbers.)

b I fill seven bags of flour each weighing 1.45 kg, from a large bag weighing 15 kg. What weight is left?

c Ask your child to say whether there is no chance, a half-chance or a certainty that:

   I will never be born.
   I will live till I die.
   'Heads' will turn up when I flip a coin

d > means more than (bigger than), < means less than (smaller than). Tell your child to use the number line and say if the following are correct or not:

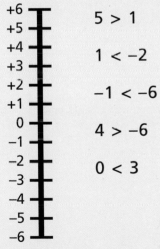

   $5 > 1$

   $1 < -2$

   $-1 < -6$

   $4 > -6$

   $0 < 3$

e ½ km = ___ m   ¼ km = ___ m

   ¾ km = ___ m   ½ cm = ___ mm

   ¼ cm = ___ mm   14 mm = ___ cm

   150 cm = ___ m   2000 g = ___ kg

No. 7

a $\frac{1}{6} + \frac{1}{6} = \frac{}{6}$

b $\frac{1}{3} = \frac{}{6}$

c $\frac{1}{3} + \frac{1}{6} = \frac{}{6}$

d $\frac{1}{2} = \frac{}{6}$

e $\frac{1}{2} + \frac{1}{6} = \frac{}{6}$

f $2\frac{1}{2} = \frac{}{2}$

g How long is it from 10.30 a.m. to 11.20 a.m.?

h How long is it from 10.45 a.m. to 13.30 p.m.?

i How many 1 cm cubes fit into a box 4 cm high, 5 cm long, and 3 cm wide?

No. 8

Finish the table and draw the block graph of the following information:

Likes of children	Tally	Number of children
Fairground rides	卌 卌 卌 ||	32
TV soaps	卌 卌	
Reading	|||	
Sports	卌 |	
Maths	||	

Which item was the most popular?
How many children took part in the survey?

Index

Acknowledgements

Executive Editor: Jane McIntosh

Editor: Emma Pattison

Design Manager: Tokiko Morishima

Designer: Mark Stevens

Illustrator: Peter Liddiard

Production Controller: Nigel Reed